DO NOT REMOVE
CARDS FROM POCKET

ALLEN COUNTY PUBLIC LIBRARY

FORT WAYNE, INDIANA 46802

You may return this book to any agency, branch,
or bookmobile of the Allen County Public Library.

DEMCO

THE ECONOMICS OF COMPARABLE WORTH

THE ECONOMICS OF COMPARABLE WORTH

MARK ALDRICH

ROBERT BUCHELE

BALLINGER PUBLISHING COMPANY
Cambridge, Massachusetts
A Subsidiary of Harper & Row, Publishers, Inc.

International Standard Book Number: 0-88730-073-1

Library of Congress Catalog Card Number: 85-26821

Printed in the United States of America

Library of Congress Cataloging-in-Publication Data

Aldrich, Mark.
    The economics of comparable worth.

    Includes bibliographies and index.
    1. Equal pay for equal work. 2. Sex discrimination against women.
I. Buchele, Robert B.   II. Title.
    HD6061.A54   1986   331.2'1   85-26821
    ISBN 0-88730-073-1

To Michele and Edith,
and Lisa and Virginia.

Table of Contents

Introduction   xix
  Notes   xxiii
  Bibliography   xxiii

Chapter 1
The Historical Antecedents of Comparable Worth   1
  Introduction   1
  Women's Earnings and Occupational Segregation   2
  Women's Work and Women's Earnings to
  World War I   3
    Jobs and Wages, 1860 to 1914   3
    Early Attempts to Improve Women's Status 6
  Progress toward Equality? From World War I to
  World War II   13
    Jobs and Wages, 1914 to 1929   13
    The Impact of Depression and War   18
  The Postwar Years: From Equal Pay to Comparable
  Worth   24
    Early Equal Pay Acts   24
    Postwar Changes in Jobs and Earnings   27
    The Rise of Comparable Worth   29
  Summary and Conclusions   33
  Notes   35
  Bibliography   35

Chapter 2
The Political Economy of Comparable Worth   40
  Introduction   40
  The Politics of Comparable Worth   40
    Comparable Worth in the Public Sector   41
    The Role of Labor Unions   42

The Legal Status of Comparable Worth   45
Job Evaluation and Comparable Worth   51
  How Job Evaluation Is Done   51
  Looney Tunes?   54
    The Subjectivity of Job Evaluation   56
    Arbitrariness of the Factor Weights   57
    Ambiguity of the Wage Equations   60
    The Role of Supply and Demand   62
  Conclusion   63
  Appendix 2–A. State Comparable Worth Activities   64
  Appendix 2–B. Comparable Worth on the Local Level   68
  Appendix 2–C. Partitioning the Wage Gap   70
  Notes   72
  Bibliography   73

Chapter 3
Sex Discrimination, Occupational Segregation, and
Comparable Worth   76
  Introduction   76
  Labor Market Discrimination   76
    Wage Theory   77
    Theories of Discrimination and Occupational
    Segregation   79
  Occupational Segregation and Comparable Worth   84
    The Crucial Role of Occupational Segregation   85
    Occupational Segregation and Women's Earnings: Is
    the Queen Wearing Any Clothes?   87
    New Findings on the Importance of Occupational
    Segregation   94
  Conclusion   100
  Notes   101
  Bibliography   101

Chapter 4
The Economic Implications of Comparable Worth   105
  Introduction   105
  A Theory of Comparable Worth   105
  Does Comparable Worth Make Economic Sense?   109
    Apples and Oranges?   109
    Supply and Demand?   110

Practice   112
Alternative Models of Comparable Worth   113
   An Advocate's Model of Comparable Worth   113
   Critique of the Advocate's Model   116
   An Economist's Model   119
   Do Women Choose Lower-Paying Jobs?   124
Conclusion   127
Notes   129
Bibliography   131

Chapter 5
The Distributional Impact of Comparable Worth   133
   Introduction   133
   Women's Jobs and Women's Earnings   134
     An Overview   134
     Models and Definitions   136
   The Impact of Comparable Worth   136
     The Impact of Comparable Worth on Selected
     Groups   137
   Comparable Worth and the Distribution of Labor
   Earnings   143
     Impact on the Overall Distribution of Wages   144
     Impact on the Black/White Wage Ratio   146
   Conclusion   146
   Appendix 5–A. Women's Employment and Earnings
   in Occupations That Are More Than 70 Percent
   Female: 1980   150
   Notes   152
   Bibliography   153

Chapter 6
The Impact of Comparable Worth on Employment   154
   Introduction   154
   The Employment Effects of Legislated Wage Increases
   in Theory   155
   The Evidence on Employment Effects   157
     Minimum Wage Laws   157
     Comparable Worth Down Under   159
   Models of Employment and Relative Earnings   160
     Wages and Employment within Jobs   160

Interoccupational Changes in Wages and
Employment   162
Combined Employment Effects   163
The Impact of Employment Changes on Women's
Earnings   169
Conclusion   170
Notes   170
Bibliography   171

Chapter 7
Conclusion   171

Index   177

About the Authors   181

List of Figures

3–1. Matching Jobs and Workers   78
3–2. Employers' Taste for Discrimination and Women's Earnings   80
4–1. The Compensating Wage Differential or Marginal Return to Job Trait   107
4–2. Sex Discrimination and Compensating Wage Differentials   108
4–3. Effect of Percent Female in an Occupation on Men's and Women's Wages in the Occupation   122

List of Tables

1–1.   Women's Relative Weekly Earnings in
       Manufacturing, 1820 to 1905   4
1–2.   Trends in Occupational Segregation, 1870 to
       1970   5
1–3.   The Feminization of Clerical Work, 1870 to 1920   6
1–4.   Determinants of Women's Relative Earnings,
       1890 to 1950   10
1–5.   Women's Relative Earnings, 1914 to 1951
       (weekly earnings in manufacturing unless
       otherwise noted)   15
1–6.   Industrial Segregation by Broad Industry Group,
       1910 to 1972   17
1–7.   Annual Earnings and Occupational Distribution
       of Men and Women, 1890 to 1930   19
1–8.   Annual Earnings and Occupations of Men and
       Women 1955 to 1980 (year-round full-time
       workers)   28
1–9.   Unionization of the Labor Force, by Sex, 1956 to
       1985   32
2–1.   Willis Associates' Point Ranges for Basic Job
       Factors in Washington State   53
2–2.   Regressions of Earnings and Job Worth Points:
       Coefficients (and t-statistics)   55
2–3.   Mean Values and Definitions of Variables
       Employed in Job Worth Regressions   56
2–4.   Why Don't These Women Earn More?   58
2–5.   Effect of Alternative Weighting Systems on Job
       Evaluation Scores by Race and Sex   59

3–1.	Occupational Segregation in the Earnings Gap	89
3–2.	The Effect of the Interaction Term on Alternative Estimates of the Impact of Occupational Segregation (a hypothetical example)	90
3–3.	Definitions of Variables	96
3–4.	Means of Variables	97
3–5a.	The Effect on Men's Wages of Percent Female in the Occupation (Dependent Variable: Mean Male Wages in the Occupation)	99
3–5b.	The Effect on Women's Wages of Percent Female in the Occupation (Dependent Variable: Mean Female Wages in the Occupation)	100
3–6.	Effect on the Male/Female Wage Gap of Distributing Men and Women Equally across All Occupations	100
4–1.	Mean of Variables	114
4–2.	Occupational Wage Equations: Advocate's Model (Dependent Variable: Mean Wages in the Occupation)	116
4–3.	Partitioning the Occupational Wage Gap: Advocate's Model	117
4–4.	Almost Women's Work: Selected Occupations That Would Not Qualify under a 70 Percent Cutoff	118
4–5.	Comparable Worth Wage Adjustments	123
4–6.	The Relationship between Percent Female in an Occupation and Undesirable Working Conditions	127
5–1.	The Distribution of Women, Women in Female-Dominated Jobs, and Women in Low-Wage Female-Dominated Jobs across Broad Occupational Groups in 1980	135
5–2.	Comparable Worth Wage Adjustments for Workers in Selected Occupations	138
5–3.	The Average Effect of a Comparable Worth Wage Adjustment for Workers in Female-Dominated Occupations	140

5–4. The Average Effect for All Workers of a
      Comparable Worth Wage Adjustment for
      Female-Dominated Occupations versus an
      Adjustment for All Occupations   141
5–5. The Impact of Comparable Worth on
      Female/Male Wage Ratios   143
5–6. Impact of Alternative Comparable Worth Wage
      Adjustments on the Distribution of Labor
      Earnings   145
5–7. Impact of Comparable Worth on the Distribution
      of Labor Earnings among Women Workers   147
5–8. The Impact of Comparable Worth on Black and
      White Wages   148
5–9. The Impact of Comparable Worth on
      Black/White Wage Ratios   149
6–1. Determinants of Male and Female Employment
      within Occupations   161
6–2. Changes in Female Employment within Broad
      Occupational Groups Due to a Comparable
      Worth Wage Adjustment   163
6–3. Translog Cost Share Equations for Broad
      Occupational Groups, and Predicted
      Employment Changes from a Comparable Worth
      Wage Adjustment for All Occupations   166
6–4. Translog Cost Share Equations for
      Female-Dominated and Other Jobs, and
      Predicted Employment Changes from a
      Comparable Worth Wage Adjustment for All
      Occupations   167

Preface

This book grows out of our dissatisfaction with much of the existing literature on comparable worth. Whether or not it will prove to be "the women's issue of the 1980s," it seems to have become a rhetorical battleground with advocates portraying their opponents as bigots and critics denouncing comparable worth as looney tunes. Although academic writing on comparable worth has usually been more polite than this, it has not been much more helpful. Economists view advocates of comparable worth as economic illiterates and largely confine themselves to denouncing it as an unwarranted interference with the laws of supply and demand. Advocates concentrate on strategies for implementation, write to each other, and ignore their critics. Politics rules the debate in the almost complete absence of serious economic analysis.

We are not so naive as to claim objectivity in this debate, but like Harry Truman's famous two-handed economist, we think there is some merit on both sides, and we have tried to be even-handed in our assessment. We do not share the world view of many economists who seem to think economic inequality is just a corollary of free choice, as if there were no such thing as discrimination in labor markets. But we are also critical of current formulations of comparable worth that potentially adjust women's wages for much more than sex discrimination. We develop a model of comparable worth that we believe is consistent with both the principles of comparable worth and of mainstream economics, and we provide some estimates of its likely impact.

We hope that this book will help readers sort out and evaluate the various claims and counterclaims in the comparable worth debate, but we are under no illusion that we have written the last word on the subject. We are certain that our analysis can be improved, and we hope critics from both sides will wish to do so.

As everyone who has co-authored a book knows, it can be both a stimulating and frustrating experience. We have not always seen eye to eye on these issues, and we continue to differ on a number of points. In spite of that fact, all parts of this book bear the imprint of both authors. They also reflect the assistance of others whose help we wish to acknowledge. We greatly appreciate Smith College's financial aid for research assistance and the unlimited computer time made available to us. Michele Aldrich, Susan Carter, and Mike Carter read parts of the manuscript and raised many searching questions that helped improve the final product. Roger Kaufmann provided able econometric advice at several points in the analysis. Frank Ackerman helped us think through an econometrics problem one Sunday morning. Carol Jusenius Romero and Jane Sommer bombarded us with academic and popular literature on comparable worth that we might otherwise have missed. Many individuals provided computer and research assistance including especially Dee Weber Burden, Chris Karem, Betty Nanartonis, Sally Powell, and Letitia Sloan. While all of these individuals have made this a better book than it would otherwise have been, they are, as usual, not to be held accountable for its views or its remaining errors. By long tradition we aggregate these to ourselves.

Mark Aldrich
Robert Buchele

Introduction

In 1955, the first year in which the Census Bureau began to publish such data, the ratio of women's to men's full-time year-round median annual earnings was 64 percent. By the early 1960s it had fallen to 60 percent.[1] In 1963 Congress passed the Equal Pay Act, which forbids pay discrimination by sex for substantively equal jobs, and in 1964 it passed the Civil Rights Act, Title VII of which prohibits sex discrimination in all employment practices, including hiring, firing, promotion, and compensation.

For the next fifteen years the earnings ratio hovered between 58 and 60 percent, showing no upward trend. And to the women who actually lived this experience, matters must have appeared even worse. In 1960 women age 25 to 34 were earning 65 percent of what men in that age group earned. Twenty years later in 1980 these women (now age 45 to 54) were earning only 54 percent as much as men in that age category (O'Neill 1985:S95). To add insult to injury, full-time, year-round female professionals earned less than male semiskilled blue-collar workers, and female college graduates earned less than male high school graduates who had never attended college. In a society as conscious of credentials and status as ours, women must have wondered why their educational and occupational attainments paid off so poorly in the labor market. It is hardly surprising that many feminists and their supporters concluded that equal pay and antidiscrimination legislation have been inadequate.

Of course, reality is more complex than this. There is evidence that equal pay and antidiscrimination requirements have had some positive impact. Women's share of employment in such relatively high-paying professions as accounting, computer science, engineering, law, and medicine has risen impressively. In this light, the constancy of the female/male wage ratio seems increasingly paradoxical, and this paradox has generated a minor industry of academics attempting to explain it. Usual approaches relate differences in men's and women's pay to differences in age, hours worked, education, and experience, but they are rarely capable of accounting for as much as half of the gap. Other academic studies of occupational segregation have demonstrated sharp differences in the male and female occupational distributions, and wage studies that include occupations are usually more successful than those that do not.

Recent history plus these academic findings seem to suggest to many observers the following diagnosis of the pay gap. First, most of the disparity between men's and women's earnings is inexplicable by anything other than discrimination. Second, the equal pay and antidiscrimination statutes have not had a large impact on women's earnings because most women continue to work in women's jobs and hence are largely unaffected by equal pay legislation. Third, it follows that raising the pay of women in women's jobs is the only policy likely to have a measurable impact on women's earnings in the near future. Given this diagnosis, the prescription seems clear: equal pay for jobs of *comparable worth*.

Although our own research is based on 1980 labor market surveys, we are aware that recently published earnings data have in fact shown a marked improvement in the female/male earnings ratio, which increased for full-time, year-round workers from 59 percent in 1981 to almost 64 percent in 1983—the level it had attained in 1955. Unfortunately, this has resulted not from an acceleration in women's wage growth but from a deceleration in men's wage growth. Thus, between 1970 and 1981 current dollar earnings of full-time, year-round workers rose by the same rate (7.7 percent per year) for both men and women. But from 1981 to 1983 women's earnings continued to grow at 7.7 percent per year, while men's earnings growth fell to 3.9 percent. This decline in male wage growth is related to the decline of male-intensive, highly unionized jobs in basic manufacturing that has occurred in recent years. While the fact that women have avoided the decline in nominal wage growth that men have experienced represents a relative gain for women, the fact remains that this gain has come about primarily as a result of the deterioration of the labor market for men, rather than the improvement of the labor market for women.

Chapter 1 provides a historical survey of women's relative earnings, occupational segregation, and public policies bearing on these issues. We find that occupational segregation has declined and the pay gap has gradually narrowed over the very long haul, but we find little evidence that changes in the male/female wage ratio have been closely associated with changes in occupational segregation. We also evaluate some of the public policies that have ostensibly been designed to benefit women workers. Critics of comparable worth have claimed that it would reinforce patterns of occupational segregation, and whether or not this is true, it is surely the case that some of the earlier attempts to improve women's status have stemmed from an impulse to control rather than liberate women's participation in the labor force. Even as late as the 1940s some advocates of comparable worth argued that federal comparable worth legislation would protect workers in male jobs from female competition.

From this historical survey of women's employment and earnings and public policy affecting them, we turn in Chapter 2 to the present efforts to implement comparable worth. We begin with a review of the legal issues involved in current federal court cases in which advocates seek to read comparable worth into Title VII of the Civil Rights Act. We share most observers' pessimism about the ultimate success of this approach and suggest that comparable worth is more likely to be implemented by state legislatures (in state and local governments) and through collective bargaining, and we review recent developments in these areas. Comparable worth as it has actually been applied is described and evaluated in the second half of this chapter. We show that the usual systems of job evaluation do not adequately measure the full range of job content and that commonly used statistical techniques arbitrarily attribute any unaccountable differences between men's and women's earnings to sex discrimination.

The motivation for comparable worth is the perception that sex-segregated jobs and the devaluation of women's work are the sources of the pay gap, and these contentions are evaluated in Chapter 3. We begin with a brief review of economic theories of discrimination and occupational segregation. We then show that while advocates of comparable·worth seem to feel that occupational segregation is the key to the pay gap, the evidence for this point is surprisingly thin. Our own estimates of the effect of occupational differences between men and women suggest that they are far less important a cause of male/female earnings differences than most supporters of comparable worth seem to believe.

We begin Chapter 4 by arguing that comparable worth can be defined in ways that are consistent with basic economic principles. Thus, we interpret comparable worth not as equal pay for comparable jobs (as advocates have tended to define it in practice) but rather as equal returns to comparable job and worker traits. So defined, comparable worth is simply the demand for an efficient, nondiscriminating labor market—a demand that neither violates the laws of supply and demand nor requires some metaphysical comparison of apples and oranges, as critics of comparable worth have charged.

But comparable worth may be implemented in ways that don't make economic sense. We specify a typical economic model employed by advocates and demonstrate that it is vulnerable to critics' charges and would be likely to yield a bogus comparable worth correction. But bogus or not, it could be employed, and we estimate the impact of its application on an economywide level. We then estimate an "economist's model" that eliminates only the part of the occupational wage differential that is associated with differences in the gender or sex composition of occupations. We find that an economywide elimination of such occupational wage differentials would raise wages in women's jobs by 10 to 15 percent, an estimate that is in fact consistent with estimates from the advocate's model and actual experience where comparable worth has been implemented.

Chapter 5 employs these findings to investigate the effects of comparable worth on the income distribution. Critics have charged that comparable worth represents an elitist vision of the world that would primarily benefit relatively well-paid white women in middle-class jobs at the expense of poorer women and black workers. As we show in Chapter 2, given the tendency of job evaluation systems to "devalue" blue-collar job traits, these charges may not be entirely without foundation. Nevertheless, our estimates of the distributional impact of comparable worth cast doubt on critics' charges that it would exclusively (or even disproportionately) benefit upper-income groups.

Specifically, we find on the basis of our model that while professional women would be major beneficiaries of comparable worth, so would relatively low-paid clerical and blue-collar workers. Only the lowest-paid group of all—retail sales and service workers—seem to be left out. Black women benefit as much as white women, and the wage distribution, both among all workers and among women workers alone, is made more equal.

Finally, in Chapter 6 we attempt to estimate the employment effects of the implementation of comparable worth on an economywide level. As a point of departure we characterize this issue as similar to the question of the potential negative employment effects of minimum wages and develop models similar to those used in the minimum wage studies. Our tentative conclusion is that comparable worth wage adjustments of the magnitude contemplated in this study would cause minor reductions in women's employment in all jobs and in the employment of all workers in "women's jobs." We estimate these disemployment effects to be much smaller than the positive wage effects of comparable worth, suggesting a net positive effect on the total earnings of workers who receive comparable worth wage adjustments.

NOTES

1. All data cited in this introduction are from the *Current Population* reports series P-60, unless otherwise noted.

BIBLIOGRAPHY

O'Neill, June. 1985. "The Trend in the Male–Female Wage Gap in the United States." *Journal of Labor Economics* 3 (Jan.):S91–S116.

CHAPTER 1

The Historical Antecedents of Comparable Worth

The Americans have applied to the sexes the great principle of political economy . . . by carefully dividing the duties of man from those of woman. . . .

ALEXIS DETOCQUEVILLE
Democracy in America, 1835

INTRODUCTION

Even the most casual survey of U.S. history indicates that women have always worked at "women's jobs" and earned women's wages. But women's work has not remained the same from the Revolution to Ronald Reagan, and women's earnings, relative to men, have risen gradually, if unevenly, from the time of their entrance into the factory system until now.

The demand that women's jobs receive "comparable worth" is part of the second great wave of concern over women's wages and work—the first having arisen during the Progressive era and resulted in protective legislation governing women's wages and working conditions. Comparable worth stems from a particular reading of women's employment and labor history that stresses the importance of occupational segregation as the source of women's relatively low pay. Like the Progressives, who mostly took the occupational structure as they found it, advocates of comparable worth do not challenge occupational segregation but rather seek to remedy its effect on women's wages by raising wages in female-dominated jobs. As a public policy, this has no historical parallels outside of wartime, with the possible exception of minimum wage legislation. But it has deep roots in both personnel administration and the ideology of the labor movement that emphasizes "the wage for the job, not the worker," and would in fact hook these horses to a feminist wagon.

This chapter sketches out some salient features of the history of women's work, paying special attention to relative earnings and occupational distributions and to public policies that affect them. As will be shown, women's relative earnings have risen gradually but unevenly over the past century and a half, while occupational segregation has declined slowly but also unevenly over the same span of history. But while this is true, it is also the case that there is little, if any, connection between changes in earnings and occupational segregation over shorter periods. Inferring changes in women's relative economic status from either of these broad indexes is, therefore, a dubious business at best.

WOMEN'S EARNINGS AND OCCUPATIONAL SEGREGATION

The average earnings of women (men) can be expressed as their earnings in each occupation, weighted by the fraction of all women (men) in that occupation. That is,

$$\overline{W}^f = \Sigma_i W_i^f O_i^f$$
$$\text{and } \overline{W}^m = \Sigma_i W_i^m O_i^m$$

where $\overline{W}^f$ and $\overline{W}^m$ are the average earnings of men and women, W_i^f and W_i^m are their earnings in occupation i, and O_i^f and O_i^m are the percentage of all women and men, respectively, in occupation O_i. Women's relative earnings therefore depend on their earnings within each occupation, compared to men and on the distribution of men and women across all occupations.

The most common measure of occupational segregation is a Duncan index:

$$I = \tfrac{1}{2} \Sigma_i |O_i^m - O_i^f|$$

Clearly, the occupational distribution affects women's relative wages. But changes in occupational segregation as measured by this index bear no necessary relation to changes in women's relative earnings. Specifically, declines in occupational segregation need not raise women's relative earnings. If there were a relatively large flow of women from a more to a less segregated occupation that paid little more for women, while at the same time a decline in the proportion of women in a highly paid occupation occurred, women's relative earnings could fall as occupational segregation declined. Clearly, the overrepresentation of women in low-paying jobs reduces women's relative earnings. But low pay relative to men within occupations may be just as important a problem. Likewise, reducing occupational segregation can raise women's relative earnings, but it is not the only potential source of increase, and it need not have this result at all. With these insights in mind, we turn to the historical record.

WOMEN'S WORK AND WOMEN'S EARNINGS TO WORLD WAR I

During the eighteenth and nineteenth centuries in the United States the demand for wage labor expanded with the gradual rise of production for markets. Factory production of textiles started in Rhode Island in the eighteenth century and employed whole families for its labor force. This system largely failed to take hold, however, for male workers had the option of being farmers. Until the great wave of Irish immigration in the 1840s created a class of workingmen too penurious to take up agricultural pursuits, few men could be induced to enter the factories. Instead, the Lowell system, which staffed the unskilled mill jobs almost exclusively with young single women, became the model for early U.S. industrialization. Male factory workers, during the antebellum years, were relatively rare and usually performed the more skilled tasks such as dyeing, finishing, and machine repair. But women constituted a majority of U.S. textile factory operatives throughout the nineteenth century. Occupational segregation and low wages for women's work were thus the very bedrock on which U.S. industrialization was built (Ware 1931; Dublin 1979; Goldin and Sokoloff 1984; Gordon, Edwards, and Reich 1982).

JOBS AND WAGES, 1860 TO 1914

Sketchy figures on women's relative earnings exist for the antebellum period, and somewhat more adequate data exist from 1860 on. They are presented in Table 1–1. Women earned about 53 percent of men's wages in 1860—sharply more than they had

Table 1–1. Women's Relative Weekly Earnings in Manufacturing, 1820 to 1905.

Year	New England and Mid-Atlantic	United States
1820	.30–.37	
1832	.41–.42	
1850	.44–.52	
1860	.53	
1861	.57	
1862	.56	
1863	.48	
1864	.43	
1865	.50	
1870	.53	
1875	.58	
1880	.63	
1890		.54
1900		.54
1905		.55

Source: 1820–50 from Goldin (1984); 1860–80 computed from data in Mitchell (1903, 1908). National data for 1890–1905 from U.S. Bureau of the Census (1903) and U. S. Bureau of the Census (1907).

several decades earlier. Their earnings fell behind those of men during the Civil War but then rose relative to male wages throughout the 1870s. These data reflect the earnings of men in a reasonably large spectrum of industries and occupations, but for women they are drawn almost entirely from the textile industry. The improvement in women's relative wages therefore reflects a rise in the relative earnings of unskilled textile workers, not a decline in occupational or industrial segregation. In fact, earnings ratios within narrowly defined occupations (weaver) rise more than the overall ratio. However, it may be that increased intraoccupation equality during these years resulted from declines in occupational and industrial segregation (discussed below) that reduced the supply of women workers in the traditionally female occupations. In all events, differentials within occupations seem to have narrowed across a broad range of

Table 1–2. Trends in Occupational Segregation,[a] 1870 to 1970.

Year	Broad Groups	Narrow Occupations
1870	54.1	
1880	48.4	
1890	46.6	
1900	39.6	64.3
1910	32.3	66.4
1920	43.2	65.7
1930	47.8	68.4
1940	46.9	68.9
1950	43.5	67.3
1960	41.7	64.9
1970	37.6	61.6

a. Duncan indexes.
Source: Column 1 from U.S. Women's Bureau (1947) and U.S. Bureau of the Census (1975: Series D 182–252); column 2 from England (1981).

women's jobs. For example, female teachers' earnings rose relative to male teachers during this period (Mitchell 1908).

Relatively complete data on employment by occupation do not exist before 1870 and by industry before 1910. Almost certainly, however, industrial segregation declined throughout the nineteenth century. For example, in 1850 about a quarter of all women (outside of agriculture) worked in the cotton textile industry, while less than 10 percent of women worked in this industry in 1900 (Abbott 1924). Moreover, several industries "tipped" from male to female or vice versa during these years. Thus, the proportion of workers in boot- and shoe-making who were female declined for a time after 1850 with the introduction of the sewing machine, while cigar and cigarette making became increasingly female dominated (Abbott 1924). The silk industry, on the other hand, gradually replaced women and especially children with male workers after 1870 (U.S. Bureau of Labor 1911 IV).

Highly aggregative data on occupational segregation in Table 1–2 and on the relative feminity of clerical work in Table 1–3 suggest that women were flowing into new patterns of work. As

Table 1–3. The Feminization of Clerical Work, 1870 to 1920.

Year	Relative Femininity of Clerical Work[a]	Percentage of Women in Clerical Work
1870	.16	.1%
1880	.28	.3
1890	.98	2.1
1900	1.32	4.0
1920	2.32	18.7

a. Percentage of clerical workers that are female divided by percentage of labor force that is female.
Source: U.S. Women's Bureau (1947) and U.S. Bureau of the Census (1975: Series D 182–252).

these figures make clear, clerical work went from being highly masculine as late as 1880 to overwhelmingly feminine work by 1910. Earnings data for manufacturing show no increase after 1880 that could be attributed to the rise of clerical work. Still, the broadening of the female occupational distribution throughout the entire nineteenth century—of which clerical work is but one example—probably accounts for part of the long-term rise in women's relative earnings that Table 1–1 documents. Late-nineteenth century textile manufacturers, for example, regularly complained of shortages of women workers in the face of "large" wage increases (Abbott 1924:143).

EARLY ATTEMPTS TO IMPROVE WOMEN'S STATUS

It seems reasonable to conclude, on the basis of the fragmentary data presented above, that women's industrial and occupational distribution broadened and their relative earnings improved throughout the last half of the nineteenth century. Earnings of factory workers may, however, have stagnated for a time after 1890, as data in Table 1–1 indicate. Almost certainly, however, earnings of all women must have continued to rise relative to men throughout this period as the great influx of women into clerical jobs that were higher paying than factory work must have raised the average of women's to men's earnings. Whatever the source of Progressive reformers' concern with women workers in the years after 1900, it could not have been their worsening economic position.

The Progressive reformers at the turn of the century focused on women workers as part of a broader concern with the impact of laissez-faire industrialization on U.S. society. Many of these reformers were leisure-class women, and they were the first generation of their class to grow to maturity in an industrial society. What they saw was crime, poverty, disease, great masses of new immigrants with unfamiliar customs, and the waste of natural and human resources on a grand scale. Industrial capitalism was transforming an older America into something new and frightening.

The Progressives responded by rejecting laissez-faire market control in favor of social control guided by informed experts like themselves (Hofstadter 1955; Hays 1957, 1969; Haber 1964; Wiebe 1967). The result was a massive array of studies of working-class life and a set of policies that would conserve older ways from the corrosive effects of free enterprise. Natural resource conservation, nativist immigration restriction, scientific management, and the protection of women and children as the future of "the race" were all policies that flowed from this world view (Hays 1969; Woodward 1951; Pickens 1968; Aldrich 1975).

The concern with conservation, broadly interpreted to include human as well as natural resources, and the desire to substitute expert for market judgments, unified much Progressive thinking (Hays 1969; Wiebe 1967). The movement for scientific management that would scientifically design jobs, set wages, and allocate labor was advertised as a way to increase output and reduce waste, while being "fair" to both employer and employee (Haber 1964). Job evaluation, although not applied to women's work during this period, became a regular feature of large firms' wage-setting practices, to be embraced eighty years later by the comparable worth movement.

Given such interests, it is not surprising that Progressives were largely uninterested in equal opportunity for women workers. Equal pay, moreover, was seen less as an end in itself than as a means to achieve Progressives' goals in areas relating to morality, poverty, and the health of women workers (and their ability to propagate the race).[1]

Unions too supported social legislation to protect women. In 1868 the National Labor Union declared itself in favor of equal pay for equal work, while a decade later the Knights of Labor issued a similar pronouncement (Commons 1918 I:436). There is no doubt that unions viewed such legislation as a way to protect male jobs and wages from low-wage female competition. In this concern they were joined by many of the leisure-class reformers who feared that women workers, by lowering men's wages, would undermine the home. Labor also shared the broader humanitarian concerns that motivated other reformers, but whatever its motives, its role in passing protective legislation was minor compared to that of middle- and upper-class groups (Steinberg 1982).

Why women earned so little in comparison to men was a question that preoccupied Progressive reformers just as it does contemporary women's groups and labor economists. Then, as now, poverty, disease, the breakup of the family, even white slavery seemed to result from the earnings gap. Explanations for women's relatively low pay that were offered at this time have a surprisingly modern ring:

Women thus are a distinct class of wage earners. They are as a group young and inexperienced . . . they stay in industry a comparatively brief time, too brief to reach the maximum earnings possible . . . they cannot rely to any extent upon a strong organization to promote their interests; . . . and . . . their economic status in the family . . . contributes a further restriction. . . . [In addition] custom and tradition . . . dictate the offer of lower wages to women than to men and put definite limits to their occupational opportunity (Hutchinson 1919: 66).

There is plenty of evidence that women's earnings at this time were not simply due to their relative youth and lack of skills and other forms of "human capital" but resulted as well from "custom and tradition." However, evidence on whether occupational and industrial segregation were a major cause of women's relatively low pay is surprisingly mixed.

Evidence from the silk and glass industries suggests that low pay did not result from women's relative youth because young women actually earned more than young men (Aldrich and Albelda 1980). However, this situation reversed at about age 16, since age and experience did not pay off as well for women as for men. This low payoff to age and experience probably came about because women were largely excluded from the skilled jobs within these industries. Apparently, it did not come about because girls who expected to spend a relatively short time in the labor force *chose* occupations with relatively high earnings at the outset but with little training potential:

the girls were engaged in nine of the 13 occupations, while boys were found in only four . . . [including] two of the simplest occupations. The girls were employed in occupations requiring considerable skill (U.S. Bureau of Labor 1911:IV 55).

Additional data from the silk industry reveal that women's earnings did rise sharply with experience (age) when they were in skilled jobs, but less so when they were in semiskilled occupations with less training potential. Moreover, the more female intensive the job in the silk industry, the lower were women's earnings (Aldrich and Albelda 1980).

These findings pertain to the silk industry, and it is hard to know how typical they may be. Although 60 percent of male workers in cotton textiles worked at jobs in which there were no women, occupational segregation does not seem to have reduced women's wages within that industry (Aldrich and Albelda 1980).

Nor is there evidence that industries that were female intensive necessarily paid women less than other industries. Data on the silk, glass, and cotton textile industries reveal no significant interindustry wage differentials after controlling for workers' jobs and personal traits. Yet half of all cotton textile workers were women, while only 8 percent of glass workers were female (U.S. Burreau of Labor 1911: I, III). Similarly, time series regressions reported in Table 1–4 that relate women's relative wages by industry to the percentage of workers that were female fail to show any significant effect of industrial segregation for the period 1890 to 1939. Other equations (not shown) based on these same data but relating men's and women's absolute wages to the percentage of industry employees that were female also fail to show any significant impact.

While evidence for the impact of occupational or industrial

Table 1–4. Determinants of Women's Relative Earnings, 1890 to 1950[a].

Group	Dep Var*	Period	Area	Trend	U/LF	%F	WWII
Manufacturing production workers	Wage	1900–50	PA, NJ	.002 (2.71)	.002 (1.91)	—	—
Office workers	Wage	1900–50	PA, NJ	.001 (1.93)	.001 (1.10)	—	—
All manufacturing workers	Wage	1890–1939	U.S.	.004 (3.63)	—	.011 (.28)	—
All manufacturing workers	Wk Earn	1890–1939	U.S.	.003 (2.69)	—	-.005 (-.16)	—
Manufacturing production workers	Wage	1914–48	U.S.	.002 (3.7)	-.002 (2.2)	—	-.05 (3.9)
Manufacturing production workers	Wk Earn	1914–48	U.S.	.003 (4.4)	.0002 (.23)	—	-.07 (4.5)

a. The dependent variable in each case is female relative to male wages or earnings. Figures in parentheses are t-ratios; %F is the percentage of industry employment that is female.

Source: Equations (1) and (2) from Phillips (1982). Equations (3) and (4) are based on data in U.S. Bureau of the Census (1903), U.S. Women's Bureau (1938), and "Women in Industry" (1938). All variables are weighted by $\sqrt{n}$. Equations (5) and (6) are derived from the National Industrial Conference Board data in U.S. Bureau of the Census (1975: Series D 833–38). These figures are average wages in twenty-five manufacturing industries weighted by the share of employment in 1923.

segregation is mixed during this period, there is a strong presumption that women were especially vulnerable to employer monopsony. In the Pennsylvania silk industry, for example, employers consciously attempted to locate no more than one plant in a town so as not to spoil the market (Chittick 1913). Such employer cartels must have been especially effective in reducing women's ability to bargain for higher wages because of their extreme geographic immobility. Consider the following evidence from the glass industry:

Women glass workers are so far from being a completely mobile labor force that even moderate mobility is rather uncommon . . . In such a situation there is no strong force at work to bring women's wages to a single level, even within a comparatively limited territory (U.S. Bureau of Labor 1911 III:406).

In fact, variations in women's wages for a given occupation in the glass industry averaged 100 percent between the highest- and lowest-paying factory within a fifty-mile radius (U.S. Bureau of Labor 1911: III, 408).

These generalizations are based on studies of factory workers. But by the late nineteenth century, factory jobs were no longer the major source of growth in women's employment: White-collar (sales and clerical) work was the wave of the future. Data presented in Table 1–3 indicate how rapidly clerical work became a female occupation. Yet even as clerical work was becoming feminized, it represented a major gain in women's occupational opportunities and helped account for the decline in occupational segregation during this period.

There is no mystery in why clerical jobs became women's work so fast. Just as women had a "comparative advantage" over men in factory work versus farming in the early years of the nineteenth century (that is, they were more disadvantaged in farming than in factory work), so they could earn relatively better wages than men in white-collar than in blue-collar jobs at the end of the century.

For middle-class women with a high school education, clerical work was ideal. It was socially more acceptable, cleaner and less arduous, as well as better paid than factory work. For employers, who would have had to pay men the equivalent of skilled blue-collar wages, women were a cheaper alternative. As a result, the enormous expansion of office employment that stemmed from the introduction of the typewriter and the rise of the large, bureaucratic corporation became predominantly female work (Davies 1975). Similarly, as the economy shifted increasingly to service work, sales clerking in the expanding department stores also became part of women's sphere (Carter and Prus 1982).

Although factory work was to become increasingly less important as a source of employment for women in the twentieth century, it occupied center stage for Progressive reformers. The movement to improve women's working conditions included attempts to prohibit women from certain kinds of employment, limit hours, prohibit nightwork, and require minimum wages. Other policies included support for vocational education that was confined exclusively to women's jobs. In addition, broader aspects of Progressive reform were also designed to help women: The safety campaign in industry was in part motivated by a desire to reduce the "need" for women to work (U.S. Bureau of Labor Statistics 1918).

Most of these policies resulted in some form of protective legislation. Beginning with an 1867 Massachusetts law that limited hours for women and children, states increasingly passed legislation regulating women's employment conditions and fixing minimum wages. Although state and federal courts initially struck down many of these laws as unconstitutional, the Supreme court, in *Muller v. Oregon* (208 U.S. 412, 1907), finally upheld the right of states to legislate in this area (Baer 1978).

There are interesting parallels between this legislation and modern proposals for comparable worth. As we have stressed, protective legislation was part of a larger movement to substitute social control by informed experts for laissez-faire. The results—minimum wages for women in combination with restrictions on employment and nightwork—must have had the effect of raising earnings in women's jobs and increasing occupational segregation, which was exactly what reformers desired. In addition, the minimum wage laws, at least, appear to have reduced employment in some cases (Peterson 1959). Thus, protective legislation constituted a mixed blessing to women workers.

Comparable worth would raise earnings in women's jobs, and possibly decrease employment in them, but its impact on occupational segregation is unclear because both men and women would have greater incentives to enter women's work. Paradoxically, however, comparable worth would help accomplish one of the Progressives' primary and most conservative goals: It would reduce the competition of women for men's jobs.

PROGRESS TOWARD EQUALITY? FROM WORLD WAR I TO WORLD WAR II

National concern over women workers faded after World War I. Even so, the three decades after 1914 apparently witnessed real, if uneven, progress for women. Major gains occurred during World War I demonstrating that the market can indeed erode discrimination if labor shortages are severe enough. And in the 1930s, a labor surplus engendered unprecedented public hostility toward women workers, resulting in public policies aimed at driving women out of the labor force. World War II resulted in major improvements in women's relative pay and occupational choices, and these gains were not entirely eroded with the war's end. By 1945 women workers faced a postwar labor market with significantly better opportunities and relative pay than any previous generation.

JOBS AND WAGES, 1914 TO 1929

World War I resulted in some major short-term occupational gains for women workers and allowed them to move into jobs that had been the exclusive preserve of men. The improvements were most spectacular for black women, who were finally able to gain a foothold in previously all-white bastions such as steelmaking and railroads. Their jobs in these industries were usually among the hardest, dirtiest, and most poorly paid that employers had to offer. But they must have been an improvement over laundry work, domestic service, and chopping cotton, since black women took to them in droves (Greenwald 1980).

Similar, although less dramatic, shifts occurred in the occupational distribution of the white female labor force. War always results in a relative expansion of metalworking industries, and this was an area in which women had previously been poorly represented. Wartime pressures forced open key apprenticeship programs—often in the teeth of resistance from male unions. Large numbers of women, attracted by the promise of skilled work at higher wages than were being paid in textiles, clothing, and sales work, endured the harassment and entered these industries (Greenwald 1980; U.S. Women's Bureau 1920).

In this century war has regularly stimulated national concern over the level of women's wages—probably because inequality and calls for sacrifice do not mix well—and in World War I both the War Labor Board and the U.S. Railway Administration pushed for equal pay for equal work. How successful these efforts may have been is not known. Women's relative earnings declined during the Civil War, but they may have risen during World War I, as the data on average weekly earnings in Table 1–5 indicate. These figures are derived from Conference Board surveys of manufacturing workers by industry. The data were then aggregated with Census-derived weights, and while the weighting process may be somewhat suspect, most of the industries from which these data were constructed also showed relative weekly wage gains for women.

The end of the war returned matters to normalcy—or almost so, because the beachhead women had achieved in new industries was not wholly wiped out. The prewar enthusiasm for reform did not survive the war and the postwar red scare however, and after one last gasp that resulted in the nineteenth amendment to the Constitution, public concern with women's social and economic problems receded. Reformers continued to press their causes, and the Women's Bureau of the Labor Department still issued pamphlets revealing the progress made by women workers. But one searches the 1920s in vain for the kind of widespread public concern with women workers evidenced only a decade earlier. It was, as the press announced, a "new era," and the Supreme Court nicely set the tone for the decade when, in 1923, it invalidated a minimum wage law for women apparently on the theory that giving women the vote ended the state's obligations to protect them (Baer 1978).

In spite of the low ebb of reform, women workers did not lose ground in the interwar years, and their relative position may

Table 1–5. Women's Relative Earnings, 1914 to 1951 (weekly earnings in manufacturing unless otherwise noted).

| Year | United States | Illinois | | Ohio Clerical |
		All	Manufacturing	
1914	.54			.60
1915				.60
1916				.59
1917				.58
1918				.57
1919	.57			.57
1920				.59
1921				.58
1923				.59
1924			.58	.59
1925			.57	.59
1926			.57	.59
1927			.57	.58
1928			.56	.58
1929			.56	.58
1930			.58	.58
1931			.59	.58
1932			.58	.58
1933			.57	.59
1934			.60	.58
1935			.59	.58
1936		.57	.57	
1937		.54	.56	
1938		.56	.57	
1939	.59	.55	.57	
1940		.55	.56	
1941		.54	.56	
1942		.53	.55	
1943		.56	.57	
1944		.59	.60	
1945		.59	.62	
1946		.63	.66	

Table 1–5 *continued*

| Year | United States | Illinois | | Ohio Clerical |
		All	Manufacturing	
1947	.50	.64	.66	
1948	.49			
1949	.49			
1951	.44			

Source: Data for 1914 and 1919 are wage data from National Industrial Conference Board (1919, 1920), weighted by estimates of industry employment by sex from U.S. Bureau of the Census (1923). Illinois data are from Illinois Department of Labor (1948: Table 3–5). Ohio clerical workers in all industries and are from U.S. Women's Bureau (1938). U.S. data for 1939 and 1947–51 are annual wage and salary earnings for full- and part-time workers in all industries from U.S. Bureau of the Census (1943) and Current Population Reports (1947–51).

have improved. The Illinois data in Table 1–5 on women's relative earnings in manufacturing industries show no apparent trend during this period. But other data—although covering a longer time span—suggest that women's relative earnings may have risen in this period. The Conference Board assembled information on women's relative earnings in twenty-five manufacturing industries with 1923 employment weights for 1914 and from 1920 to 1948. In addition, there are variable weight data on specific industries for several states from 1900 to 1950, while a third data set (already noted) contains information on relative wages and occupational segregation from 1890 to 1937. These data have been used to test for time trends in women's relative earnings. As the results in Table 1–4 indicate, a significant positive trend appears to exist both for factory and office workers. The findings suggest that the ratio of women's to men's wages was rising at about two to three percentage points per decade. These results are quite robust: They hold for many specific industries, as well as for all industries combined, for production and white-collar workers and for daily wages as well as weekly earnings.

There appears to be only a loose connection between the course of women's relative earnings during these years and either industrial or occupational segregation. As data in Table 1–6 indicate, industrial segregation declined from 1910 to 1940.

But since industrial segregation was apparently not associated with women's relative earnings (see Table 1–4), this decline cannot explain wage trends. Occupational segregation, on the other hand, fell from 1870 to 1900 or 1910—depending on which index one consults—while women's relative earnings rose. But from 1900 to 1910 through 1930 or 1940, segregation increased at the same time that women's relative earnings continued to rise.

Table 1–6. Industrial Segregation by Broad Industry Group, 1910 to 1972.

Industry Group	Ratio of Percentage of Females in Industry to Percentage of Females in Labor Force		
	1910	1940	1972
Agriculture, forestry, fisheries	.42	.49	.47
Mining	.01	.04	.18
Construction	.02	.05	.15
Manufacturing	.90	.87	.74
Transportation, communication, public utilities	.19	.38	.53
Wholesale and retail trade	.97	1.13	1.11
Finance, insurance, real estate	.63	1.38	1.31
Business and repair services	.02	.30	.74
Personal services	16.46	7.80	1.95
Entertainment	.98	.77	.94
Professional	3.58	3.85	1.65
Government	.30	.74	.78
Duncan index	46.10	38.90	42.60
Duncan index (manufacturing only)	46.90	38.60	34.60

Note: Data are the percentage of the industry that is female divided by the percentage of the labor force that is female.

Source: Data for 1910 and 1940 from Palmer and Ratner (1949). Data for 1972 from U.S. Bureau of Labor Statistics (1982) and U.S. Bureau of the Census, *Current Population Report* (1972).

It is possible to separate the changes in women's relative earnings that were due to shifts in the occupational distribution from those that resulted from changes in relative earnings within occupations. Table 1-7 presents earnings by occupation for broad occupational classes for 1890 and 1930. As can be seen, the female to male earnings ratio rose from about 46 percent to 56 percent over this period. The next row, W_f/W_m (1890), shows what these ratios would have been had 1890 wages rates obtained in 1930. As can be seen, about 70 percent of this increase resulted from changes in wages within occupations, with the remaining 30 percent due to changes in the occupational distribution—even as actual occupational segregation increased.

As Table 1-7 makes clear, the most important occupational shifts for women were their relative flow out of service and farm occupations and into sales and clerical work. But it was the rise in women's relative earnings *within* these broad occupational groups rather than occupational shifts that accounts for most of their relative gain. Moreover, the relative pay increase for clerical workers could not have been due to changes in occupations within this broad group, for as Niemi (1983) has shown, most of the pay differences between male and female clerical workers resulted from unequal pay on the job, not differences in the job distribution. Williamson and Lindert (1980) have argued that the wage premium for skills remained largely unchanged over this period. If so, then the rise of women's relative pay within occupations probably did not result from any narrowing of intragroup skill differentials but may instead have reflected rising relative skill levels for women. Whatever may have been the causes, the female to male pay ratio for professional and managerial employees rose from 26 percent to 36 percent over this period; for clerical and sales workers it rose from 49 percent to 71 percent; and for the other groups in Table 1-7 it rose from 53 percent to 57 to 60 percent.

THE IMPACT OF DEPRESSION AND WAR

The Great Depression seems to have had little impact on women's relative earnings, if the Illinois data in Table 1-5 are to be believed. With women earning little more than half of men's wages, employers must have been sorely tempted to substitute

Table 1-7. Annual Earnings and Occupational Distribution of Men and Women, 1890 to 1930.

	1890 Male		1890 Female		1930 Male		1930 Female		1955 Male		1955 Female	
	Earnings	Distribution	Earnings	Distribution	Earnings	Distribution	Earnings	Distribution	Earnings	Distribution	Earnings	Distribution
Professional	$1,500	9.0%	$366	10.3%	$3,712	13.6%	$1,428	16.5%	$5,555	24.9%	$3,333	18.5%
Clerical	943	2.2	459	2.1	1,566	5.5	1,105	20.9	4,248	7.2	3,109	41.3
Sales	943	3.8	456	2.6	1,580	6.1	959	6.8	5,205	5.5	3,394	5.5
Manual	498	31.1	268	25.2	1,523	45.2	868	19.8	4,237	45.8	2,570	18.8
Service	445	3.2	236	39.9	1,220	4.8	730	27.5	3,674	5.6	1,434	15.6
Farming	445	50.7	236	19.9	1,220	24.8	730	8.4	1,339	10.9	940	1.7

Female to Male Earnings Ratios

	1890	1930	1955
W^f/W^m	.456	.556	.652
W^f/W^m (assuming 1890 wages and current year occupational distribution):	.456	.485	
W^f/W^m (assuming 1930 wages and current year occupational distribution):	.456		.526

Source: Goldin (1984). Goldin used the 1900 occupational distribution for 1890; this table uses an 1890 distribution derived from U.S. Women's Bureau (1947).

women for men wherever possible, thereby reducing labor costs and worsening male unemployment. This possibility at least was the specter feared by many at the time. In an era of job shortages, employment of women was seen as taking jobs away from men who presumably needed them more to support their families (Scharf) 1980). To prevent such an undesirable result, even such liberals as Eleanor Roosevelt urged to women to stay home.

In addition, the National Recovery Administration took the position that paying women less than men for "equal work" was an unfair competitive practice. Just as in the Progressive Era, the push for equal pay aimed to prevent women's employment in men's jobs as much as it did to raise women's earnings. In fact, nearly two-thirds of the over 500 NRA codes contained some form of clause requiring equal pay for women (Schneiderman 1939; U.S. Women's Bureau 1935). Equal pay provisions combined with the minimum wages set under the codes and later under the Fair Labor Standards Act often raised women's wages more than those of men. Studies of the silk and rayon and the woolen and worsted industries done by the Bureau of Labor Statistics reveal increases in wages for both men and women and a sharp increase in women's relative earnings (Hinrichs 1935; Tolles 1935). Similarly, data comparing men's and women's weekly earnings in nineteen New York industries in 1931 and 1934 show that women's average earnings rose from 52 percent to 59 percent of the men's wages—a statistically significant increase (U.S. Women's Bureau 1935). The irony of these events should not be overlooked. Progressives had pushed for minimumum wages for women partly to reduce their employability. Yet in 1928 the Women's Bureau had argued that minimum wages for women did not reduce their employment (U.S. Women's Bureau 1928). Finally, only seven years later the same policies were again instituted in part to achieve that very end.

The NRA codes and minimum wages may have reduced women's employment prospects, but at least they raised wages. Other public policies had fewer blessings. The Works Progress Administration was the largest single federal source of work relief, and its policies toward women reveal some of the ways social and occupational norms of the 1930s affected women workers. Faced with more applicants than it could employ, the WPA instituted screening criteria that, while ostensibly race and sex neutral, in fact were sharply detrimental to both women and black workers. First, it instituted a "breadwinner" policy of denying relief to "secondary" wage earners. Second, it limited the time an individual could be on the rolls to eighteen months. Such "neutral" behavior as this, because it forced individuals back into a labor market that discriminated by race and sex, was itself discriminatory. Moreover, when in spite of these policies the rolls still contained "too many" women, they were occasionally simply purged. As a result, while women constituted about 22 percent of the labor force in 1930, they typically amounted to only 13 to 16 percent of WPA workers (Howard 1943).

There is also the matter of what women on the WPA rolls did. Just as turn-of-the-century reformers who advocated vocational education for women were unable to push beyond the stereotypical female occupations of that day (and as CETA would sixty years later repeat the same pattern), so WPA officials in the 1930s confined women to women's work. Over half of all women on WPA roles worked on sewing projects, and qualified women were rejected when "suitable" projects for them could not be found (Howard 1943). With women confined to such trades and paid "prevailing wages," there was probably little danger that they would later be employed on male jobs.

While the Great Depression seems to have had little net impact on women's relative earnings and occupations, the same was not true of World War II. There is nothing like a tight labor market to shake up established employment practices, and World War II created what may have been the tightest labor market in U.S. history. Almost immediately women workers shifted from being a national liability to one of the country's greatest assets. As *Fortune* magazine put matters in 1943: "The Margin Now Is Womanpower" (1943:99). Subsequent research would underline this insight. Britain and the United States, in the face of unprecedented demands for labor, overcame many of the stereotypes of women's proper duties and employed then effectively in the war effort. Nazi Germany, mired in nineteeth-century notions about hearth, home, motherhood, did not (Rupp 1978).

Occupational and industrial segregation were early casualties of the war effort: In no similar period in U.S. history have the patterns of women's work changed so drastically. One index of industrial segregation (not shown) declines from 48.4 in 1939 to 29.4 in 1944 (U.S. Bureau of Labor Statistics, Employment Statistics Division 1945). While these industries are somewhat less aggregative than those on which the manufacturing indexes in Table 1–6 are based, comparisons are still possible, and industrial segregation clearly fell more in this five-year period than it did from 1910 to 1972. Durable goods production—a nearly all-male preserve in 1939—integrated with a vengeance under the pressure of wartime labor shortages and by 1944 employed almost its "share" of women. Within the durable goods sector, industries such as aircraft and parts, which had been male bastions in 1939, employed nearly as many women as men by 1943. No data exist to chart the course of women's occupations during the war, but segregation surely declined as the new women workers in these industries worked as craftsmen and operatives—jobs in which women were historically underrepresented.

As in World War I, patriotism also required a policy of equal pay. In 1942 the War Labor Board issued General Order 16 allowing equal pay for equal work for women workers. There was, however, less here than met the eye. First of all, the order *allowed* but did not require equal pay. Second, it applied only within (not between) plants, and only to women who replaced men in men's jobs (Nationl War Labor Board 1945).

General Order 16 probably did help raise some women's earnings, but it clearly did not mandate equal pay for equal work. Several surveys of women workers in "men's" jobs revealed widespread lower starting rates, and occasionally flatter experience/earnings progressions for women than for men in the same job (National Industrial Conference Board 1943; U.S. Women's Bureau 1944; New York State Department of Labor 1944).

It is hard to tell what impact the national commitment to equal pay, such as it was, had on women's relative earnings. The information on earnings that exists for World War II is quite fragmentary. Significant negative coefficients on the WWII dummy in fixed employment weight regression equations reported in Table 1–4 suggest that women's relative earnings declined. Yet the

Illinois data in Table 1–5 indicate a rise in both weekly earnings and hourly wages. Analysis of these data indicates—unsurprisingly—that wages rose fastest in industries where employment increased most sharply. Thus, while women's relative earnings within industries may actually have declined, the shift in female employment to (increasingly) high-wage work offset this effect, thereby raising women's relative pay.

The experience of women's relative earnings during these years is instructive. It suggests that short-term changes in the pattern of demand can result in sharp changes in relative earnings and employment by occupation that may swamp adverse intraoccupational wage changes. It also highlights a point raised by conservative critics of comparable worth: that relative wages depend on supply and demand conditions, as well as on job requirements. How, one wonders, would the economy have reallocated labor as effectively as it did, if wage increases in "male" jobs had required wage increases in female jobs to maintain their comparable worth?

It is impossible to know for sure whether women's earnings improved or declined compared to that of men in the whole period from the 1930s through World War II because adequate data simply do not exist. Census estimates of earnings of full-time workers begin only in 1955, and these are contained in Table 1–7. When compared with the 1930 figures in that table, they suggest a sharp rise in women's relative pay over this quarter century (although how much of this may have occurred in the decade between 1945 and 1955 is not known).

This progress resulted entirely from an increase in women's relative pay within broad occupational groups. As the bottom row of Table 1–7 shows, if relative earnings within occupations had remained at their 1930 levels, changes in occupations alone would have reduced women's relative earnings, although segregation actually fell from 1930 to 1950. This rise in women's relative earnings probably resulted in part from their rising labor force experience, since married women's average experience rose from about nine years to over 10.5 years from 1930 to 1950 (Goldin 1984). A second possible cause of rising intraoccupational wages for women was the decline in skill premiums during this period (Williamson and Lindert 1980). Such declines may have disproportionately benefited women who tended to be in the least-skilled jobs within occupational groups. In addition, Goldin (1984) has argued that because men shifted into professional work more rapidly than women during this period, its declining wage premium reduced the impact of this shift on women's relative wages.

THE POSTWAR YEARS: FROM EQUAL PAY TO COMPARABLE WORTH

As we know, the end of the war sent "Rosie the Riveter" back home. But it did not erode all of the wartime gains that women made into new occupations and industries. In 1939 women constituted less than 1 percent of all production workers in transportation equipment. This figure rose to 22 percent by 1944, and it still remained at 7 percent in 1947. Women rose from 5 percent of all production workers in machinery in 1939 to 20 percent in 1944, and then declined to 9 percent in 1947 (U.S. Bureau of Labor Statistics, Employment Statistics Division 1945; U.S. Women's Bureau 1952).

EARLY EQUAL PAY ACTS

Just as World War II left a lasting imprint on women's work, so it also made its mark on laws affecting their pay. Between 1943 and 1946, Illinois, New York, Massachusetts, and Washington passed some form of equal pay acts, although like much previous and subsequent state legislation, most of them seem to have been narrow and unenforceable. And in 1945 the first of what would prove to be a very large number of equal pay bills with broad coverage was introduced into the U.S. Congress.

These early federal equal pay bills would, if passed, have enacted something very much like industrywide requirements for equal pay for comparable worth. This was clearly the goal of their supporters. Discussing the Equal Pay Act of 1946, one advocate argued that

The scientific rating and classification of jobs appear to offer a basis for proving that the historic differentials between women's occupations and men's occupations are discriminatory (Brady 1947:57).

Similarly, the 1948 version of the act (H.R. 4408) forbid sex discrimination:

(1) for work of comparable character on jobs the performance of which requires comparable skills; or

(2) for comparable quality and quantity of work on the same or similar operations (U.S. Congress 1948).

One supporter of the bill, Ruth Roemer of the United Electrical Workers (IUE), made it clear that she thought the bill mandated comparisons across jobs:

We are not only talking here about the same rate of pay on the same job. . . . In addition, we are talking about historic differentials where it is a comparable job, requiring comparable quality and quantity of production, or comparable character of jobs, the performance of which would require comparable skills (U.S. Congress 1948:205).

In addition to its broad definition of equal work, the bill also allowed the Secretary of Labor to set up industrywide committees to study and make recommendations on the elimination of sex-based wage differences throughout each industry. On the basis of such recommendations, the secretary was authorized to find the differential an unfair labor practice.

Clearly, this was an ambitious bill. Its supporters included a large number of women's groups and labor unions, as well as members of the Women's Bureau. They argued that such a bill was necessary because increasing numbers of women were self-supporting and unable to earn a living wage. In addition, advocates appealed to newly popular Keynesian notions, claiming that raising women's wages would enhance purchasing power. The third major argument for the bill echoed claims of Progressives and NRA supporters. "For men," Helen Gahagen Douglas argued, "this bill will help sustain wage rates because it will discourage employers from hiring women as wage cutters" (U.S. Congress 1948:15).

Not surprisingly, labor unions also stressed this point in their testimony. While equal pay within plants would have helped protect male jobs, the provision for *industry* committees would have been even more important to labor because it could have reduced North/South wage differentials based on sex and therefore helped solve the problem of runaway shops.

Supporters of the bill argued that wages should be set on the basis of job evaluation studies and that there should be a rate for the job. In fact, testimony showed that job evaluation procedures, which were embraced in the Progressive Era to enhance worker efficiency, were increasingly being adopted by large firms. However, these firms usually employed job evaluation as part of a process that linked "key" jobs to market wages—which resulted in different earnings schedules for male and female occupations. This was the sort of thing supporters thought the bill should prevent. Committee members, however, saw the specter of a vast federal program that would rank all jobs from ditch digger to president and substitute the judgment of government agents for that of businesses:

Mr. McConnell (Rep. Pa). This will be difficult to administer. . . . Do you not feel this will require a job classification for the entire country?

Mrs. Douglas (Rep. Calif.). I think it would be worked out on job classification and job evaluation. I believe that is something most industries do anyway.

Mr. McConnell. No. I don't know. I don't see how you can get at this unless you have a complete job classification all over the United States (U.S. Congress 1948:27–28).

Some of the arguments over the bill are precisely those that arise in modern debates over comparable worth.

Mr. Fisher (Rep. Tex.). . . . [Suppose] there is a man stenographer who has been there the same length of time as a lady stenographer, both of them write the same number of letters per day and work the same length of time, but because of the lady's pleasing personality and perhaps her contacts with other people . . . he is paying her, say $250 per month and paying the man only $200. Then this law becomes effective and there might be a question as to whether the employer would be forced to reduce the woman's salary to the $200. . . .

Mrs. Douglas. Well, as you describe this young woman, she seems to be a public relations person as well as a stenographer. They wouldn't be doing comparable work. . . .

Mr. Fisher. Who will determine which one is doing the most from the standpoint of public relations, the employer or Uncle Sam? (U.S. Congress 1948:23–24).

POSTWAR CHANGES IN JOBS AND EARNINGS

Whether women's relative earnings in the early postwar years responded to these legislative concerns is not entirely clear because, as noted above, data on earnings of full-time employees are unavailable before 1955. Census figures on the ratio of female to male median wage and salary incomes for full- and part-time workers combined (in Table 1–5) reveal a decline from 1947 to 1951, however. And median wage and salary data for full-time workers indicate that relative female wages stagnated during the late 1950s and then declined.

These trends in relative wages do not seem to have stemmed from any corresponding trends in the occupational distribution, however. As Table 1–2 indicates, segregation seems to have declined from 1940 to 1970. Moreover, additional data indicate that occupational segregation declined between 1960 and 1980 (Beller 1985), and a broad index of segregation is uncorrelated with women's relative earnings (Albelda 1983).

Why then did this pause occur in what has otherwise been a steady, if slow, rise in women's relative earnings? Data in Table 1–8 present earnings and occupational distributions for men and women for broadly defined occupations from 1955 to 1980. The actual ratio of women's to men's earnings is presented as is the ratio computed using current occupational distributions and the earnings of the initial year. Comparison of the bottom two rows of Table 1–8 shows that changes in the occupational distribution reduced women's relative earnings *although occupational segregation was declining*. This continues the trends of 1930 to 1955, precisely reversing events of the 1890 to 1930 period when about 30 percent of the increase in women's relative earnings came from occupational shifts at a time when occupational segregation was rising.

After 1955 the male occupational distribution continued to shift as it had in the 1890 to 1955 period toward professional, managerial, and crafts occupations and away from farming and laboring. The most dramatic change in women's occupational distribution was the shift from operatives to managers, and this

Table 1-8. Annual Earnings and Occupational Distribution of Men and Women, 1955–1980 (year-round full-time workers).

| | 1955 | | 1955 | | 1960 | | 1960 | | 1980 | | 1980 | |
	Male		Female		Male		Female		Male		Female	
Professional	$5,668	10.2%	$3,559	12.1%	$7,228	12.9%	$4,550	12.3%	$23,026	17.6%	$15,285	19.4%
Management	$5,477	14.7	2,851	6.4	6,922	17.2	3,535	6.7	23,558	18.2	12,936	10.1
Clerical	4,248	7.2	3,109	41.3	5,328	7.6	3,645	41.1	18,247	6.2	10,997	39.3
Sales	5,205	5.5	3,394	5.5	5,938	6.2	2,397	5.6	19,910	6.1	9,748	4.4
Crafts	4,766	18.8	3,107	1.3	5,905	19.5	3,602	1.0	18,671	21.5	11,701	2.1
Operatives	4,117	20.4	2,532	17.5	5,030	18.1	3,021	15.5	15,702	15.4	9,440	10.4
Service	3,674	5.6	1,434	15.6	4,209	6.1	2,115	15.6	13,097	6.9	7,767	12.7
Labor	3,104	6.6	2,204	.3	3,959	4.5	2,415	.4	12,757	4.2	9,747	1.0
Farm*	1,339	10.9	940	1.9	2,129	8.2	1,316	1.6	7,763	3.6	4,726	.5

Ratio of Women's to Men's Earnings

	1955	1960	1980
W/W^m	.652	.610	.602
W/W^m (assuming 1955 wages and current year occupational distribution):	.652	.619	.619

*Includes farm managers and farm labors.

Source: Computed from data in U.S. Bureau of the Census, *Current Population Reports*, Series P-60, various years. Where data on women's earnings were unavailable, the ratio for all occupations applied to men's earnings in the occupation was employed.

had a relative minor impact on earnings—perhaps as a result of the erosion of skill premiums during the years (Williamson and Lindert 1980).

Although the earnings of female relative to male managers and professionals rose during these years, some changes in intraoccupational wages eroded women's pay compared to men. Perhaps because women's schooling and experience declined compared to men during this period (O'Neill 1985), the pay of women clerical workers fell from 73 percent to 60 percent of men, while female sales workers saw their earnings diminish from 65 percent to 49 percent of men.

THE RISE OF COMPARABLE WORTH

During the 1920s and 1930s the status of women workers was not a matter of great public concern. However, World War II stimulated the passage of several equal pay acts, and when the war ended public interest in women workers did not immediately die out. Instead it seems to have grown steadily stronger.

As noted above, federal equal pay acts were submitted annually from 1946 on, and between 1946 and 1953 seven states plus Alaska passed some form of equal pay law. From 1955 to 1965 another sixteen states passed equal pay or fair employment practice laws. In 1952 a National Committee for Equal Pay was formed. The AFL had endorsed the principle of equal pay as long ago as 1898; in 1956 it came out in favor of a federal equal pay act.

Finally, in 1963, after eighteen years of efforts, the Federal Equal Pay Act was passed. The final version of the act was much narrower than the immediate postwar bills. The sections setting up industry councils were long gone, thereby ensuring that the bill would apply only within firms. And the language of the bill was much narrower than the earlier acts. Gone were provisions mandating equal pay for jobs of comparable value or skill, and instead the act required equal pay "for equal jobs the performance of which requires equal skill, effort, and responsibility." Nor was this change of language an accident. According to Congressman Goodell, a sponsor of the bill,

We went from "comparable" to "equal" meaning that the jobs involved would be virtually identical. . . . We do not expect the Labor Department to go into an establishment and attempt to rate jobs that are not equal. . . . (quoted in Golper 1983:565).

Pretty clearly, Congress, knew what it wanted when it passed the Equal Pay Act, and it did not want comparable worth.

The next year Congress prohibited employment discrimination by race and sex in Title VII of the Civil Rights Act. The history of these acts and their enforcement throughout the 1960s and 1970s is complex. They have clearly helped open many previously all-male jobs to women and have probably reduced occupational segregation and raised some women's earnings (Beller 1979, 1982). But they obviously do little if anything for women currently in or entering female jobs. And even while overall measures of occupational segregation have registered declines, a large fraction of women workers continue to work in such traditional jobs as clerical work and the "helping professions." As a result, two decades of experience with equal pay, equal employment, and affirmative action have resulted in no noticeable impact on the female/male earnings ratio.

At the same time that these acts were being passed and implemented, the economics profession rediscovered women workers. Up through the 1950s labor economics had been dominated by institutionalists who concerned themselves largely with labor unions and their impact. But in the early 1960s human capital explanations of individual workers' earnings became more fashionable, and the old institutionalist concerns faded into relative obscurity.

By the middle 1960s economists began to try to explain male/female earnings gaps by differences in the amounts of schooling, experience, and other "human capital endowments." Literally dozens of such estimates have been generated, and they usually find that at least half (often much more than half) of the wage gap is left unexplained—potentially the result of discrimination.[2]

In the early 1970s a renaissance of institutionalist thinking occurred as some economists began to stress that labor markets were segmented by industry, occupation, race, and sex (Doringer and Piore 1971). This led to further studies of the wage gap that emphasized the importance of women's segregation into low-wage occupations (Stevenson 1975; Jusenius 1976; Roos

1981). Studies that included occupations as well as human capital variables accounted for a much higher fraction of the wage gap, while other research seemed to show that women's returns to human capital were lower in female jobs.

At the same time that economists were discovering discrimination and occupational segregation, women's rights activists were drawing some of their own conclusions about the male/female earnings distribution. The stagnation in women's relative earnings and the continuing fall in skill premiums resulted in sharp declines in the pay of women sales and clerical workers relative to blue-collar craft occupations. Given the frequency with which comparable worth advocates compare the pay of blue-collar male jobs with white-collar female jobs, it appears that the erosion in earnings and status of these jobs probably accounts for some of moral outrage characterizing the pay equity movement.

To women's rights advocates, the conclusion seemed clear: Laissez-faire resulted in discrimination and occupational segregation, while past efforts at social intervention such as equal pay and affirmative action laws were inadequate. Apparently, no policy that ignored the problem of low pay in these female-dominated jobs could hope to have a measurable impact on women's earnings—at least not over any reasonable period of time.

Some of these conclusions also appealed to the U.S. labor movement, which had its own reasons for emphasizing women's issues. Organized labor has been declining both as a political and an economic force since the middle 1940s. The relative growth of white-collar and nonmanufacturing employment—both of which have remained largely unorganized—played some role in labor's decline. In addition, the movement of industry into the South and, in the 1970s and 1980s, deregulation and the rise of import competition have all eroded unionization. And so has the rising fraction of the labor force that is female. As the data in Table 1–9 indicate, only about 15 percent of women workers were organized as late as 1973—about half the male percentage. With unions' base among male workers eroding, and with female workers comprising a growing percentage of the labor force, organizing women has become a union imperative.

Some unions at least have risen to the challenge. Findings by

Table 1–9. Unionization of the Labor Force by Sex, 1956 to 1983.

	1956	1966	1973	1980	1983
Percentage unionized					
Labor force					
Females	14.9	12.6	14.5	16.7	16.1
Males	31.0	29.7	32.7	30.3	24.2
Public sector					
Females			17.3	32.3	38.1
Males			28.0	38.8	39.2
White collar					
Females			10.4	15.6	15.8
Males			11.4	17.5	15.9
Percentage of union workers who are female					
Total	18.5	19.3	23.7	31.7	40.7
Public sector			36.7	47.3	46.7
White collar			44.3	54.6	58.2

Source: Freeman and Leonard (1984).

Freeman and Leonard (1984) plus our own work in Chapters 3 and 4 below suggest that unions have generated relative pay benefits for women. Perhaps for this reason, as Table 1–9 reveals, unions have been more successful with women workers than with men in the past decade, and big gains have come among white-collar, female, and public-sector employees. Over half of all white-collar workers and nearly half of all public-sector employees who are in unions are women. It is no surprise then that many of the unions that grew rapidly during the 1960s and 1970s were those that were most successful in organizing women. For example, State, County, and Municipal workers (AFSCME) more than doubled its membership between 1966 and 1978, while women members rose from less than 5 percent to 40 percent of the total. The American Federation of Teachers (AFT) experienced similar growth and feminization. The Service Employees (SEIU) grew by two-thirds, and an increasing fraction of its members also were women. The American Federation of Government Employees grew more slowly, but nearly all of its new membership was female (U.S. Bureau of Labor Statistics 1977, 1979).

Given these patterns of labor force participation, employment shifts, and declining union membership, self-interest clearly dictated that labor emphasize its benefits for women workers. And while these circumstances made comparable worth expedient, trade union history and ideology all made it deeply appealing. As noted, labor organizations have supported equal pay legislation for women since the days of the National Labor Union. Partly this has been to prevent low-wage competition from women workers, but it also fits in well with the labor movement's commitment to egalitarian social reform. In addition, when marshalled in the service of feminist goals, labor's belief that wages adhere to the job, not the person, and its long experience with and support for job evaluation, almost inevitably lead it to embrace the principle of comparable worth. In fact, Council 28 of AFSCME in a 1973 letter to the governor of Washington, seems to have first raised the modern demand for equal pay for comparable work (Comparable Work Project 1984).

SUMMARY AND CONCLUSIONS

As this survey indicates, occupational segregation of women workers remains endemic, and wages are far below those of male workers. But neither relative wages nor occupational distributions have remained unchanged. Occupational and industrial segregation have declined over the very long term, but they have done so unevenly, and the long-term decline has been interrupted by shorter periods of increase. Similarly, average earnings of women workers relative to men have risen over the long term— but with interruptions. Finally, changes in women's relative earnings show little connection to changes in occupational or industrial segregation. This suggests that there may be only a loose connection between the stagnation in women's relative earnings in the 1960s and 1970s and the degree of occupational segregation. And it also suggests that policies to reduce the impact of occupational segregation—like comparable worth—may have a limited affect on women's relative earnings.

Women's employment and earnings have been matters of public concern since the 1830s or earlier, and matters of public policy since the Progressive Era. Often the reformers who wished to improve women's economic status were motivated in part by other concerns—patriotism, the war effort, the family, the Depression. Because women's position was seen as an instrument as well as a goal, public policy has not always been an unalloyed blessing to women workers. Some policies of the Progressives were designed to restrict women's choices, and nearly all advocates of equal pay up through the 1940s argued that one of its main benefits would be to protect male workers' jobs and wages. Yet these public policies have also conveyed benefits to working women. Minimum wages, although they probably reduced employment, did raise wages, and the opening up of male jobs during World War II did benefit women workers. Affirmative action and equal pay legislation in the 1960s also generated real gains for many women, even if counteracting trends offset those gains in the aggregate.

The movement for comparable worth is in some respects similar to earlier reforms. One impetus for comparable worth has been academic findings that show that a large portion of the male/female earnings gap cannot be explained by differences in education, training, experience, or job preferences. Like the massive factual studies of industrial conditions in the Progressive era, the academic studies of the 1970s provide the intellectual support for modern groups proposing to extend social control over labor markets. Along with the obvious fact of occupational segregation and the apparent failure of equal pay and affirmative action policies, academic studies support the conclusion of comparable worth advocates that raising earnings in women's jobs is the obvious solution to the problem of low wages for women.

But ideas, if they are to be translated into public policy, need a standard bearer, and in addition to academics and women's groups, organized labor has joined the cause. The concomitant stagnation and feminization of the labor movement have compelled its leaders to become increasingly receptive to ideas for improving women's economic status. And comparable worth, which would harness such old labor demands as job wages and job evaluation to pull up women's earnings, is one such idea.

NOTES

1. The connection between protective legislation and the health of future generations is made in Josephine Goldmark (1912) and Irving Fisher (1912). Fisher asserted that "the employment under improper conditions of women, especially of married women, means an even more serious waste of life and strength for future generations" (p. 3). Goldmark (p. 115) also cites Fisher as follows: "The present working day is a striking example of the failure to conserve national vitality." For arguments that the minimum wage was necessary for women workers' health, see Seager (1913) and Brown (1913).
2. A survey of labor economics journals and textbooks that were published during the 1950s reveals the institutionalist perspective that shaped research at that time. The leading voice of the human capital school, the *Journal of Human Resources* was not even founded until 1966. While articles on women's pay began to appear in the middle 1960s, the earliest such piece in the *JHR* did not appear until 1971. Thereafter, the flood of econometric wage equations began to transform all the labor journals and texts. For a survey of the literature on male/female pay differentials, see Treiman and Hartmann (1981).
3. The labor market segmentation literature dates from the work of Doringer and Piore (1971). Studies that stress the impact of occupational segregation are too numerous for an inclusive list. A representative sampling would include Stevenson (1975), Jusenius (1976), and Roos (1981).

BIBLIOGRAPHY

Abbott, Edith. 1924. *Women in Industry*. New York: D. Appleton.

Albelda, Randy. 1983. "Black and White Women Workers in the Post World War II Period." Ph.D. dissertation, University of Massachusetts, Amherst.

Aldrich, Mark. 1975. "Capital Theory and Racism: From Laissez Faire to the Eugenics Movement in the Career of Irving Fisher." *Review of Radical Political Economics* 7 (Fall):33–42.

Aldrich, Mark, and Randa Albelda. 1980. "Determinants of Working Women's Wages During the Progressive Era." *Explorations in Economic History* 17:323–41.

Baer, Judith. 1978. *Chains of Protection*. Westport, Conn.: Greenwood.

Beller, Andrea. 1979. "The Impact of Equal Employment Opportunity Laws on the Male/Female Earnings Differential." In *Women in the Labor Market*, edited by Cynthia B. Lloyd, pp. 304–330. New York: Columbia University Press.

――――. 1982. "Occupational Segregation by Sex: Determinants and Changes." *Journal of Human Resources* 17 (Summer):381–92.

――――. 1985. "Changes in the Sex Compensation of U.S. Occupations 1960–1981." *Journal of Human Resources* 20 (Spring):235–50.

Blau, Francine, and Wallace Hendricks. 1979. "Occupational Segregation by Sex: Trends and Prospects." (*Journal of Human Resources* 14 (Spring):197–210.

Brady, Dorothy. 1947. "Equal Pay for Women Workers." *Annals of the American Academy of Political and Social Science.* 251 (May):53–60.

Brown, H. LaRue. 1913. "Massachusetts and the Minimum Wage." *Annals of the American Academy of Political and Social Science* 48 (July):13–21.

Carter, Susan, and Mark Prus. 1982. "The Labor Market and the American High School Girl, 1890–1928." *Journal of Economic History* 42 (March):163–71.

Chittick, James. 1913. *Silk Manufacturing and Its Problems.* New York: James Chittick.

Commons, John R. 1918. *History of Labor in the United States.* Vol. 1. New York: Macmillan.

"Comparable Worth: The Facts and Controversy." 1984. *Quality of Worklife Review* 2 (Spring):12–18.

Davies, Margery. 1975. "Women's Place Is at the Typewriter: The Feminization of the Clerical Work Force." In *Labor Market Segmentation,* edited by Richard C. Edwards, Michael Reich, and David Gordon, pp. 279–96. Lexington, Mass.: Heath.

Doringer, Peter, and Michael Piore. 1971. *Internal Labor Markets and Manpower Analysis.* Lexington, Mass.: Lexington Books.

Dublin, Thomas. 1979. *Women at Work: The Transformation of work and Community in Lowell Massachusetts, 1826–1860.* New York: Columbia University Press.

England, Paula. 1981. "Assessing Trends in Occupational Sex Segregation, 1900–1976." In *Sociological Perspectives on Labor Markets.* edited by Ivar Berg, pp. 273–95. New York: Academic Press.

Fisher, Irving. 1912. "Industrial Hygiene as a Factor in Human Conservation." *Proceedings of the Academy of Political Science II* 18–23.

Freeman, Richard, and Jonathan Leonard. 1984, "Union Maids: Unions and the Female Workforce." Paper presented at the Conference on Gender in the Workplace, Sponsored by the Committee on the Status of Women in Economics and the Brookings Institution, Nov. 15–16.

Goldin, Claudia. 1984. "The Earnings Gap in Historical Perspective." In *Comparable Worth: Issue for the 80s* I:3–22.

Goldin, Claudia, and Kenneth Sokoloff. 1984. "The Relative Productivity Hypothesis of Industrialization: The American Case." *Quarterly Journal of Economics* 99 (Aug.:461–87.

Goldmark, Josephine. 1912. *Fatigue and Efficiency.* New York: Russell Sage Foundation.

Golper, John. 1983. "The Current Legal Status of Comparable Worth in the Federal Courts." *Labor Law Journal* 34 (Sept.):563–80.

Gordon, D.; R. Edwards; and M. Reich. 1982. *Segmented work, Divided Workers: The Historical Transformation of Work in the United States.* New York: Cambridge University Press.

Greenwald, Maurine. 1980. *Women, War, and Work.* Westport, Conn.: Greenwood.

Haber, Samuel. 1964. *Efficiency and Uplift: Scientific Management in the Progressive Era.* Chicago: University of Chicago.

Hays, Samuel. 1957. *Response to Industrialism*. Chicago: University of Chicago.

———. 1969. *Conservation and the Gospel of Efficiency*. New York: Atheneum.

Hinrichs, F. A. 1935. "Wages and Earnings in the Silk and Rayon Industry, 1933 and 1934." *Monthly Labor Review* 40 (June):1432–47.

Hofstadter, Richard. 1955. *Age of Reform*. New York: Knopf.

Howard, Donald. 1943. *The WPA and Federal Relief Policy*. New York: Russell Sage.

Hutchinson, Emily. 1919. *Women's Wages*. New York: Columbia University Press.

Illinois Department of labor. 1948. "Historical Series." *Labor Bulletin* 9 (July/Aug.):23–47.

Jusenius, Carol. 1976. "The Influence of Work Experience, Skill Requirement, and Occupational Segregation on Women's Earnings." *Journal of Economics and Business* 29:107–15.

"The Margin Now Is Womanpower." 1943. *Fortune* 27 (Feb.):99 +.

Mitchell, Wesley C. 1903. *A History of the Greenbacks*. Chicago: University of Chicago.

———. 1908. *Gold, Prices, and Wages, 1860–1880*. Berkeley: University of California.

Muller v. Oregon. 208 U.S. 412 (1907).

National Industrial Conference Board. 1919. "Wartime Changes in Wages." *Research Report* 20. Boston, Mass.

———. 1920. "Changes in Wages during and since the War." *Research Report* 31. New York.

———. 1943. "Wartime Pay of Women in Industry." *Studies in Personnel Policy* 58. New York.

National War Labor Board. 1945. "National War Labor Board Policy on Equal Pay for Equal Work for Women." *Research and Statistics Report* 32. Prepared by Ella Polinsky. Washington, D.C.

New York State Department of Labor. Division of Women in Industry and Minimum Wages. 1944. *Women's Wages on Men's Jobs*. New York.

Niemi, Albert. 1983. "The Male–Female Earnings Differential." *Social Science History* 7 (Winter):97–107.

O'Neill, June. 1985. "The Trend in the Male–Female Wage Gap in the United States." *Journal of Labor Economics* 3 (Jan.):S91–S116.

Palmer, Gladys, and Ann Ratner. 1949. "Industrial and Occupational Trends in National Employment." *Wharton Industrial Research Department Report* 11. Philadelphia: University of Pennsylvania.

Peterson, John. 1959. "Employment Effects of State Minimum Wages for Women: Three Historical Cases Re-examined." *Industrial and Labor Relations Review* 12 (April):406–22.

Phillips, Peter. 1982. "Gender-Based Wage Differentials in Pennsylvania and New Jersey Manufacturing, 1900–1950." *Journal of Economic History* 42 (March):181–86.

Pickens, Donald. 1968. *Eugenics and the Progressives*. Nashville: Vanderbilt.

Roos, Patricia. 1981. "Sex Stratification in the Workplace: Male–Female Differences in Economic Returns to Occupation." *Social Science Research* 10:-195–223.

Rupp, Leila. 1978. *Mobilizing Women for War: German and American Propaganda 1939–1945*. Princeton, N.J.: Princeton University Press.

Scharf, Lois. 1980. *To Work and to Wed*. Westport, Conn.: Greenwood.

Schneiderman, Rose. 1939. "Women in Industry under the National Recovery Administration." In *On Economic Planning*, edited by Mary Van Kleek and Mary Fledderus, pp. 163–70. New York: Covice, Friede.

Seager, Henry R. 1913. "The Minimum Wage as Part of a Program for Social Reform." *Annals of the American Academy of Political and Social Science* 48 (July):3–12.

Steinberg, Ronnie. 1982. *Wages and Hours: Labor and Reform in Twentieth Century America*. New Brunswick, N.J.: Rutgers University Press.

_____. 1984a. "Statement." In U.S. Commission on Civil Rights, *Comparable Worth: Issue for the 80's* 2, pp. 55–72. Washington, D.C.: GPO.

_____. 1984b. " 'A Want of Harmony': Perspectives on Wage Discrimination and Comparable Worth." In *Comparable Worth and Wage Discrimination*, edited by Helen Remick, pp. 3–27. Philadelphia: Temple University Press.

Stevenson, Mary. 1975. "Relative Wages and Sex Segregation by Occupation." In *Sex, Discrimination and the Division of Labor*, edited by Cynthia B. Lloyd, pp. 175–200. New York: Columbia University Press.

de Tocqueville, Alexis. 1835. *Democracy in America* (translated by Henry Reeve, 1899). 2 vols. New York: Colonial Press.

Tolles, N. A. 1935. "Wage Rates and Weekly Earnings in the Woolen and Worsted Industry, 1932–1934." *Monthly Labor Review*, 40 (June):1448–59.

Treiman, Donald, and Heidi Hartmann, eds. 1981. *Women, Work, and Wages*. Washington D. C.: National Academy Press.

U.S. Bureau of Labor. 1911. *Report on Condition of Women and Child Wage Earners in the United States* III and IV. Washington, D.C.: GPO.

U.S. Bureau of Labor Statistics. 1918 "Effect of Workmen's Compensation Laws in Diminishing the Necessity of Industrial Employment of Women and Children." *Bulletin* 217. Prepared by Mary K. Conyngton. Washington, D.C.: GPO.

U.S. Bureau of Labor Statistics. 1977. "Directory of National Unions and Employee Associations." *Bulletin* 2044. Washington, D.C.: GPO.

_____. 1979. "Directory of National Unions and Employee Associations. "*Bulletin* 2079. Washington, D.C.: GPO.

_____. 1982. "Labor Force Statistics Derived from the Current Population Survey." *Bulletin* 2096, I. Washington, D.C.: GPO.

_____. Employment Statistics Division. 1945. "Women in Factories, October, 1939–June, 1945." Mimeo.

U.S. Bureau of the Census. 1903. Census of 1900. *Special Report on Employees and the Wages*. Washington, D.C.: GPO.

_____. 1907. Census of Manufacturers. 1905. *Part I: U.S. By Industries*. Washington, D.C.: GPO.

_____. 1923. Census of Manufacturers. 1921. *Bienniel Census of Manufacturers*. Washington, D.C.: GPO.

_____. 1943. Census of Population, 1940. *Wage and Salary Income in 1939*. Washington, D.C.: GPO.
_____. 1947–80. *Current Population Reports*. Series P-60. Washington, D.C.: GPO.
_____. 1975. Historical Statistics of the United States. 2 vols. Washington, D.C.: GPO.
U.S. Congress, House Committee on Education on Labor, 80th Cong. 2d Sess. 1948. *Hearings on Equal Pay for Equal Work*. Washington, D.C.: GPO.
U.S. Women's Bureau. 1920. "The New Position of Women in American Industry." *Bulletin* 12. Washington, D.C.: GPO.
_____. 1928. "Effects of Labor Legislation on Employment Opportunities for Women." *Bulletin* 65. Washington, D.C.: GPO.
_____. 1935. "Employed Women under NRA Codes." *Bulletin* 130. Prepared by Mary Elizabeth Pidgeon. Washington, D.C.: GPO.
_____. 1938. "Differences in the Earnings of Women and Men." *Bulletin* 152. Prepared by Mary Elizabeth Pidgeon. Washington, D.C.: GPO.
_____. 1944. "Women's Wages in Wartime." n.p.
_____. 1947. Women's Occupations through Seven Decades." *Bulletin* 218. Prepared by Janet Hooks. Washington, D.C.: GPO.
_____. 1952. "Handbook of Facts on Women Workers." *Bulletin* 242. Washington, D.C.: GPO.
Ware, Carolyn. 1931. *The Early New England Cotton Manufacture: A Study in Industrial Beginnings*. Boston: Houghton Mifflin.
Wiebe, Robert. 1967. *The Search for Order, 1877–1920*. New York: Hill and Wang.
Williamson, Jeffrey, and Peter Lindert. 1980. *American Inequality: A Macroeconomic History*. New York: Academic Press.
"Women in Industry." 1938. *Monthly Labor Review* 46 (April):900–03.
Woodward, C. Vann. 1951. *Origins of the New South*. Baton Rouge: Louisiana State University Press.

CHAPTER 2

The Political Economy of Comparable Worth

[Comparable worth] would lead to a flood of litigation, massive wage redistribution, a distortion of free market principles and, ultimately, widespread job dislocation.

—HERITAGE FOUNDATION
(New York Times, Dec. 10, 1984:A10)

The bigots are stepping up their campaign to argue that it is all right to discriminate against women.

—WINN NEWMAN, AFSCME lawyer
(New York Times, Dec. 10, 1984:A10)

INTRODUCTION

As we have seen, the demand for comparable worth dates back at least to the closing days of World War II. But the modern movement seems first to have taken root in the state of Washington in the middle 1970s and has spread from there via litigation, legislation, and collective bargaining to perhaps thirty other states at the time of this writing. Comparable worth has spread primarily through collective bargaining and union-initiated lawsuits at the state and local level. Accordingly, we begin this chapter with an assessment of the role of unions in promoting comparable worth and the current legal status of comparable worth in the courts. We then turn to a critical analysis of job evaluation and the implementation of comparable worth.

THE POLITICS OF COMPARABLE WORTH

So far at least, comparable worth has been a hothouse flower that seems to blossom best within the public sector—often after some coaxing by unions and the courts. The affinity of comparable worth for the public sector is probably not accidental. Government employees are becoming increasingly highly organized, sometimes by aggressive unions with large female membership, such as the American Federation of State, County, and Municipal Employees (AFSCME). Most public-sector employers are formally committed to job evaluation as a basis for setting wages, and their employment practices are more subject to public policy than those in the private sector. Finally, public sector employers may be less sensitive to wage costs than are private employers (since their "product market" is noncompetitive) and are less likely to reduce employment if labor costs rise (Gregory and Duncan 1981; Ehrenberg and Smith 1984). The next section provides an overview of the progress of comparable worth in the public sector.

COMPARABLE WORTH IN THE PUBLIC SECTOR

Appendixes 2–A and 2–B at the end of this chapter provide some information on the spread of comparable worth as of early 1985. As can be seen, a majority of states and many cities are either studying or implementing comparable worth in some form or other. Most of the current and pending state legislation on comparable worth pertains to state and or local government employment only, although some could be applied to the private sector. So far, eight states—Connecticut, Iowa, Louisiana, Minnesota, New Mexico, South Dakota, Tennessee, and Washington —have implemented or are about to implement comparable worth for state employees. At least ten states have been involved in some sort of comparable worth litigation *(Daily Labor Report* 69 April 10, 1985; Equal Employment Advisory Council 1985).

At the federal level, there have been a number of initiatives, the most ambitious of which, such as H.R. 4599, the Federal Employees Pay Equity Act of 1984, would initiate a comparable worth study of the Federal Civil Service or, like S. 1900, the Pay Equity Act of 1983, would require comparable worth of federal contractors (Rothchild 1984). Although the immediate impact of these bills is restricted to employees of the federal government and federal contractors, they are viewed by employers as a menacing first step toward a federal comparable worth law for the whole private sector and strongly opposed by employer lobbys such as the U.S. Chamber of Commerce. As of this writing, however, it appears that comparable worth activists have been more successful in collective bargaining, litigation and lobbying at the state and local level than in getting favorable legislation at the federal level. Accordingly, we turn to a review of union comparable worth activities and then to the status of comparable worth in the courts.

THE ROLE OF LABOR UNIONS

As we argued in Chapter 1, comparable worth would seem to have a natural attraction for the labor movement. On an abstract level it appeals to ideas of fairness that unions have long advocated and even manages to equate equity with merit ("equal pay for comparable work"). It would set the wage for the job, not the worker, a time-honored principle of the labor movement, and it is a fresh approach—a rallying cry—for organizing women workers. Moreover, *all* of the recent growth in female union membership has been in white-collar and public employment, and it is here that unions seem to have benefited women most (Freeman and Leonard 1984).

Unions are also a potentially powerful ally of comparable worth activists. The union's duty of fair representation requires it to represent the interests of all the members in the collective bargaining unit (Volz and Breitenbeck 1984). The elimination of sex and race discrimination is a mandatory subject of collective bargaining, and an employer can be charged with bad-faith bargaining if he refuses to bargain over these issues. Moreover, unions have access to information (unavailable to the individual worker) on the race and sex characteristics and promotion histories of employees (Freeman and Leonard 1984). Female unionists are therefore in a position to harness their unions to the comparable worth movement, and their unions are in a unique and powerful position to carry its banner.

It is also true that comparable worth can be a potentially divisive issue for labor, pitting women against higher-paid men in the same or other unions. In some unions there has been considerable male resistance to women's demands for comparable worth *(Wall Street Journal,* Sept. 16, 1982:33). Police and firefighter unions strongly opposed being included in Minnesota's comparable worth plan. As one observer put it, "the firemen went crazy because the point system classifies a librarian's job the same level as a fireman's job" (Wall Street Journal, May 10, 1985:-27).

Yet such is the organizing potential of comparable worth that, in an increasingly female labor force, the balance of risks and benefits has tipped in its favor—at least for most unions with (potentially) large female membership. Even the AFL–CIO has gone on record supporting the concept, calling on its affiliated unions, "to initiate joint union–employer pay equity studies to identify and correct internal inequalities between predominantly female and predominantly male classes" (Portman, Grune, and Johnson 1984:225).

Yet the debate was acrimonious and served to highlight the limited appeal of comparable worth to private-sector unions. The fight for the amendment was lead by Electrical Workers (IUE), AFSCME, and the Communications Workers (CWA), all of whom have large female white-collar constituencies, and two of whom (AFSCME and CWA) have strong public-sector ties. On the other hand, the Garment Workers (ILGWU), whose membership is 85 percent female and employed in a highly competitive low-wage industry in the private sector, opposed it. President Sol Chaikin explained his reservations:

I'll be damned if I know of a way to get the women more money. The value of their work isn't set by theoretical principles but on the value of the work in the marketplace and in the face of competition from overseas, where garment workers make 30 cents an hour (Business Week Dec. 17, 1979:69).

Unions have pursued comparable worth not only in the courts—the subject of the next section—but also through collective bargaining and political pressure. Union participation in pay equity issues received an important boost when the National Labor Relations Board ruled in Westinghouse Electric Corp. (239 N.L.R.B. 106 1978) that in collective bargaining an employer must provide the union with data on the race and sex composition of all its workers (Freeman and Leonard 1984).

Similarly, AFSCME has aggressively pursued comparable worth at the bargaining table and in court. AFSCME Local 101 led the first comparable worth strike in the United States in San Jose, California. The strike erupted after a job evaluation done for the city by Hay Associates demonstrated that women in management jobs in the city received less pay than men in jobs the study had rated as comparable. The city agreed to correct these inequities, and AFSCME then demanded a similar study for non-management workers. The city agreed and commissioned a second Hay study in 1979. AFSCME demanded and won strong representation on the committee that assigned "job worth points," having discovered that, as Mike Ferraro, head of Local 101 put it, "Whoever controls the study can have an awful lot to do with its outcome" (McGuire 1982:13).

Not surprisingly, the study showed that female jobs were paid 10 to 20 percent below the average. At this point, perhaps after it calculated the costs of pay equity, the city began to drag its feet. As a result, an epidemic of "Hay fever" descended on San Jose public employees, shutting down libraries and other public facilities, and on July 5 the union formally struck the city (McGuire 1982; Farnquist and Strausbaugh 1983). After nine days, an agreement was reached: The city agreed to raise the pay in sixty-two female-dominated jobs to within 10 percent of the average for their grade.

Since the San Jose city workers' strike, pay equity has become an increasingly important collective bargaining issue. In 1982 nurses in San Jose hospitals struck, demanding a 37 percent pay increse that would raise them to the level of pharmacists (*New York Times*, Feb. 14, 1982:38; Comparable Worth Project, Winter 1982:8–10). In addition, AFSCME filed charges with the EEOC against twelve public employers and has negotiated pay equity adjustments with Santa Clara, California, and Spokane, Washington. Clerical workers in Allegheny County, Pennsylvania, and school secretaries in Anoka, Minnesota, have struck over pay equity (*Wall Street Journal*, Sept. 16, 1982:33). The first comparable worth strike to involve a private-sector employer, began at Yale University when 1,800 members of Local 34 of the Federation of University Employees, a clerical and technical union that is 82 percent female, struck for higher pay on September 26, 1984. The bitter and highly disruptive strike was suspended over the Christmas break and finally settled just before it was to be resumed in January 1985 with a new contract raising current employees' pay 35 percent over three and one-half years (Cook 1983; Rothchild 1984; *Business Week,* Nov. 26, 1984:92+; *New York Times,* Jan. 23, 1985:B2; Comparable Worth Project, Winter 1985:1+).

THE LEGAL STATUS OF COMPARABLE WORTH

As a public-sector collective bargaining issue, comparable worth is no more or less threatening to private-sector employers than, say, the Davis Bacon Act. Davis Bacon, by requiring "prevailing wages" on public construction, may raise labor costs on private as well as public projects. Similarly, as a private-sector collective bargaining issue, comparable worth could be seen as simply a slogan to capture the moral high ground for labor's side in wage negotiations. But a comparable worth law applied to the private sector is an entirely different matter, for here it involves not only money, but power.

Government shapes private-sector wage negotiations in a number of ways—for example, through minimum-wage legislation, antidiscrimination laws, and in the National Labor Relation Act requirement that employers bargain with unions in good faith. But none of these involves government in setting wages for specific private-sector jobs in the way that comparable worth threatens to do. Applied to the private sector, comparable worth would make courts or some federal agency the arbiter of companies' pay scales. As Murray Weidenbaum, former chairman of the Council of Economic Advisors under President Reagan, has said, "The comparable worth approach implies that the Government will assume the role of personnel officer" (*New York Times,* Sept. 4, 1984:B9). In short, public, not private, bureaucrats would be setting or approving wages. Advocates have been quite clear on this matter. Ronnie Steinberg, director of the Comparable Worth Program at SUNY at Albany, New York, indicated her vision to the Commission on Civil Rights:

the people who bring [psychometric, sociometric and econometric techniques] to bear on a particular problem may be able to bring enlightening findings back to a . . . legislative task force, or a court (Steinberg 1984:63).

It is surely the specter of *regulation* that accounts for the hostility that comparable worth has provoked on the right. Conservative commentators have rushed to inform public opinion with articles such as "Comparable Worth: Another Terrible Idea" (Cowley 1984) and "Comparable Worth: The Feminist Road to Socialism" (Levin 1984). Civil Rights Commission Vice-Chairman Morris Abram is apocalyptic in his vision of comparable worth leading

to permanent government wage control over a substantial if not the majority [sic], of the working population. *(Wall Street Journal* April 12, 1985:60).

And Cornell University economist George Hildebrand is apoplectic in his denunciation:

What the principle [of comparable worth] calls for is federal intervention into the occupational wage and salary structure on a very large, and possibly even massive, scale (Hildebrand 1980:102).

How likely are these visions of doom? As Appendix 2–A indicates, at least twenty-four states have some sort of law relating to comparable worth. Many have had such a statute for some time, although those that were passed before the late 1970s were usually intended to affirm the Equal Pay Act rather than to be new comparable worth legislation as it is understood today. Thus, comparable worth could be implemented nationwide either for state and local governments only, or for all employees, through state-by-state legislation. However, competition among states to establish favorable business environments will probably blunt any state-level initiative to impose comparable worth on private employers.

In theory of course, the Civil Rights Commission or the Equal Employment Opportunity Commission could take an active role in promoting comparable worth. But the EEOC has ruled unanimously that unequal pay for work of comparable value is not in itself proof of sex discrimination *(Daily Labor Report* 117, June 18, 1985). And the recent rejection of comparable worth by the U.S. Commission on Civil Rights *(Daily Labor Report* 71, April 12, 1985), indicates that intervention by this agency is also unlikely. Comparable worth has made important gains in the federal courts, though even there the outlook is clouded.

Two federal statutes prohibit sex discrimination in pay: the Equal Pay Act of 1963 and Title VII of the 1964 Civil Rights Act. The Equal Pay Act does not prohibit *all* pay differences, however. Employers may justify pay differentials based on (1) a seniority system, (2) a merit system, (3) a system basing earnings on quality or quantity of output, or (4) anything other than sex (Golper 1983:566). Title VII of the Civil Rights Act prohibits sex discrimination in employment and compensation, but Congress apparently drafted it with little thought of how it related to the Equal Pay Act. To clarify this relationship and to ensure that in the event of a conflict between the two acts, "the provisions of the Equal Pay Act shall not be nullified" (Golper 1983:566), Senator Bennett proposed what came to be called the Bennett amendment, which reads in part

It shall not be . . . unlawful . . . for any employer to differentiate upon the basis of sex in determining the amount of wages or compensation paid or to be paid to employees of such employer if such differentiation is authorized by [the Equal Pay Act] (Golper 1983:566).

Up until 1979 the federal courts had interpreted the Bennett amendment to mean that no claim would be upheld under Title VII unless it also violated the Equal Pay Act. A plaintiff claiming sex discrimination in wages under Title VII therefore had to show that the jobs involved were "substantially equal." Thus, in the famous Denver Nurses case, *Lemons v. City & County of Denver*, 620 F.2d 228 (1980), a district court rejected the plaintiffs' allegations of discrimination because they were paid less than men in comparable (but not equal) jobs. The court noted that Denver based its compensation on rates nurses received in similar communities elsewhere and declined to involve itself in a job evaluation study (Kurtz and Hocking 1983). Moreover, where the jobs involved were equal, an employer could still envoke any of the four defenses noted above.

Beginning in 1979, however, the courts began to modify this position to allow claims under Title VII even where the jobs involved did not meet the test of equality required by the Equal Pay Act. The most important of these cases to date is *County of Washington v. Gunther*, 452 U.S. 161 (1981). The plaintiffs, who were female prison matrons, were paid 70 percent of the rate paid male jail guards. The women claimed sex discrimination under Title VII, basing their claim on a salary survey by the county showing that they should have received 90 percent of the male guards' rate. A federal district court rejected their claim because male and female guards' jobs were not substantially equal, but it was reversed on appeal by the Ninth Circuit Court of Appeals, which was, in turn, upheld by the U.S. Supreme Court.

In *Gunther,* the Supreme Court read the Bennett amendment to Title VII much more narrowly than previously, interpreting it as restricting employers' legal justifications for sex-related wage differentials to the four defenses listed in the Equal Pay Act. *Gunther* thus established that claims under Title VII no longer need to pass the test of substantial equality required by the Equal Pay Act. But while this ruling broadens the range of cases that plaintiffs may successfully litigate under Title VII, it by no means throws open the doors to comparable worth. In *Gunther,* the Court found evidence of *intentional* sex discrimination on the part of the defendant, and the majority concluded that Congress (in the Bennett amendment) could not have intended "to insulate such blatantly discriminatory practices from judicial redress under Title VII" (Golper 1983:569). This is, in fact, a narrow ruling. The Court did *not* find that the existence of sex-segregated jobs was in itself illegal, and it explicity disavowed a comparable worth interpretation of its decision. It simply found that intentional pay discrimination is illegal under Title VII, even if the jobs involved are not substantially equal (Thomas 1983; Heen 1984; Siniscalco and Remmers 1984).

A potentially much broader application of Title VII, and one that if finally upheld would virtually mandate comparable worth for every employer in the country, grows out of a Washington state lawsuit: *American Federation of State, County & Municipal Employees v. State of Washington,* 33 F.E.P. 808 (1983). Like many other states, Washington rates state government jobs and sets wages to reflect rates "prevailing in other public and private employment" (Siniscalco and Remmers 1984:9). Beginning in 1974 Washington commissioned several job evaluations, all of which showed that women's jobs were usually underpaid compared to men's jobs with similar numbers of points. Former Governor Daniel Evans then requested funds of the legislature to begin implementation of comparable worth, but Dixy Lee Ray, who succeeded him, removed the funds from the budget.

In July 1982 AFSCME sued the state alleging illegal discrimination under Title VII. It cited the various job evaluation studies as evidence that the state paid workers in predominantly female job classes less than workers in predominantly male job classes "for work of comparable, equal or greater value" (Chi 1984:35). In September 1983 District Court Judge Jack Tanner found for the plaintiffs. He ordered the state to begin implementation of comparable worth and to make back pay awards that have been estimated to total $800 million or more.

This is a much more creative reading of the law than the Supreme Court undertook in *Gunther,* and its significance was not lost on Winn Newmann, lawyer for AFSCME:

If you can win in Washington State, I'm satisfied that you can win against virtually every employer. . . . Virtually every employer is guilty of the same form of sex discrimination (Siniscalco and Remmers 1984:- 15).

Judge Tanner based his findings not on evidence that the state had intended to discriminate but on the "disparate impact" of its compensation scheme which was not justified by "business necessity."[1] He also refused to accept the state's claims of flaws in the job evaluation studies that purported to show unequal pay for comparable worth. Although he rejected plaintiffs' claim of sex segregation as such, he concluded that it was an element supporting their contention of disparate impact.

Judge Tanner has characterized *AFSCME v. State of Washington* as a "straightforward failure to pay case" in which the state had failed to "rectify an acknowledged disparity in pay between predominantly female and predominantly male job classifications" (Siniscalco and Remmers 1984:8). In *Gunther,* the county had ignored its external labor-market wage survey in underpaying its prison matrons. In *AFSCME* the state had ignored the results of its comparable worth studies and continued to follow its market-based compensation system. The state, then, was guilty of failing to substitute a compensation system based on a comparable worth job evaluation for one based on market wages. This decision appears to make an employer that undertakes job evaluation studies and then pays some women's jobs less than comparably rated men's jobs liable under Title VII. This would seem to discourage employers from undertaking job evaluation studies that could be used against them by their employees in Title VII suits.[2]

In September 1985 the Ninth Circuit Court of Appeals systematically dismantled Judge Tanner's decision, ruling that "neither law not logic deems the free market a suspect enterprise *(Daily labor Report* 173, Sept. 6, 1985:AA–1). The Appeals Court added that "a study which indicates a particular wage structure might be more equitable should not categorically bind the employer who commissioned it. The employer should be able to take into account market conditions, bargaining demands, and the possibility that another study will yield different results" (AA –2). Finally it argued that "job evaluation studies and comparable worth statistics alone are insufficient to establish the requisite inference of discriminatory motive . . ." (AA–2). By inference, market-based compensation systems that have a disparate impact do not violate the law.

AFSCME has said that it will appeal this decision. But even if it were finally to win this case, comparable worth claims would probably be initiated through charges filed with the Equal Employment Opportunity Commission, which could then presumably investigate the charges and bring suit to require comparable worth. But the EEOC has already disavowed the disparate impact doctrine and the principle of comparable worth in a unanimous decision in June 1985. Given the views of the Reagan administration and of the people it has appointed to the Civil Rights Commission and the EEOC, it is unlikely that complaints brought to these agencies would be pursued with great zeal at this time.

But given legal encouragement and a more liberal political climate, the EEOC could at some future time be swamped with comparable worth claims. There appears to be no reason why *any* group could not file and perhaps win if the disparate impact theory were accepted. Could not women in nonfemale jobs or Hispanic males claim that their employers' pay schemes devalued their jobs? And would it not be reasonable to suppose that some white males at least would undertake a job evaluation to demonstrate underpayment for their work? Male performers in pornographic movies apparently earn only about half the pay of their female co-stars in what appear to be positions requiring "comparable" skill and effort (Friendly 1985:62). Could they sue? Who would do the job evaluation? Presumably employers would respond to all these suits by hiring job evaluation consultants of their own who had a high propensity to "find" that employers' present practices conformed to comparable worth, and the commission would then be forced to decide between contending "experts" over which is the correct measure of comparable worth.

But even if the Appeals Court decision in *AFSCME v. State of Washington* is upheld and these events fail to come to pass any time soon, comparable worth claims will simply move from federal courts to state legislatures and the collective bargaining arena, and job evaluation will still play a central role in the debate. Judge Tanner's acceptance of the studies' findings and his refusal to accept claims that the studies were flawed simply serves to highlight their importance: Comparable worth is job evaluation writ large, and it is to that topic that we now turn.

JOB EVALUATION AND COMPARABLE WORTH

In this section we describe how jobs are evaluated and how the resulting job ratings are typically used to make comparable worth wage adjustments. We then evaluate this approach, with special attention to the validity of attributing all differences in the wage equations for men's and women's jobs to discrimination.

HOW JOB EVALUATION IS DONE

Job evaluation studies can be done in a number of ways, but the most common method, and that employed in most of the celebrated comparable worth controversies, uses the point factor method (Treiman 1979; Treiman and Hartmann 1981; Schwab 1980, 1984; Remick 1984; Beatty and Beatty 1984). Such studies typically employ a panel of job evaluation "experts" to rate each job according to four or five predetermined "factors." As the San Jose AFSCME local official quoted above suggested, the composition of this panel is likely to affect the resulting ratings, and as the consultants performing the studies acknowledge (Bellak 1984), it will certainly affect the credibility of the study to those affected by it. While the San Jose panel was composed of non-management personnel, the group that performed the 1974 Washington state job evaluation study were all professional and supervisory personnel who worked in the following occupations (Willis *et al.* 1983):

Registrar
Program manager
Economist
Administrative analyst
Caseworker
Compensation analyst
Personnel specialist
Labor market analyst
Staff representaive, State Council of County and City Employees
Equal Employment Opportunity supervisor
Director, Washington State Women's Council
Registered nurse supervisor
Program analyst

These experts rate each job on a scale for each of the factors. Each factor is assigned points, and the points for each factor are summed up to arrive at a job's total score. Table 2–1 shows the point ranges in Willis Associates' studies of Washington state and the point ratings for some representative jobs.

Potential ranges for some of these categories are actually much greater than these Washington state data reveal. For example, the Hay scales for "know-how" and "problem solving" in a 1976 study of state government jobs in Idaho range from 50 to 2,432 points, while for accountability the range is from 10 to 2,-800 points. By contrast, working conditions are scored on a scale running from 0 to 66 points (Treiman 1979:App. 15).

Once jobs are rated, pay scales can then be developed, and it is at this stage that job evaluation as traditionally practiced by employers differs from the comparable worth approach. When employers use job evaluation, they typically divide the occupa-

Table 2–1. Willis Associates' Point Ranges for Basic Job Factors in Washington State.

Factor	Point Range
1. Knowledge and skills	60–280
Job knowledge	
Interpersonal skills	
2. Mental demands	8–140
Latitude for independent judgement	
Extent of decisionmaking and	
problemsolving required	
3. Accountability	11–160
Freedom to take action	
Nature of job's impact	
4. Working conditions	0–20
Physical effort	
Hazards	
Discomfort	

Job Worth Points for Selected Jobs, Willis Study of Washington State

Position	Knowledge Skill	Mental Demands	Accountability	Working Conditions	Total
Registered nurse IV	280	122	160	9	571
Caseworker III	212	92	70	10	384
Boiler operator	92	17	20	15	144
Laundry worker I	70	10	11	17	108

Source: U.S. Congress, House, Committee on Post Office and on Civil Service (1983).

tions into broad categories such as administrative, professional, clerical, blue collar, and so on. Labor-market salary surveys are then undertaken for benchmark jobs within each of these groups, and a salary is set for those jobs. Pay for the other jobs *within* the group is then interpolated by some formula that links its points and pay to those of the benchmark jobs. But no attempt to link points and pay *across* groups is made.

While this procedure could be sex-blind, it does not yield sex-neutral results because it will typically yield lower wages for a given number of job points in the female-dominated jobs than in the male-dominated jobs, and so most women will be paid less than most men. The extent of this "devaluation" or underpayment of women's work has been estimated using Willis and Hay comparable worth studies by fitting separate wage equations to data on the men's and women's jobs. Some results are shown in Tables 2–2 and 2–3, which present regression equations and means of variables for monthly salary and job worth points from the Willis study of Washington state in 1976 and the Hay study of Minnesota in 1983.

Armed with these data, we can see how a comparable worth calculation might be made. From column 1 of Table 2–2, the equation for male wages in Washington state is:

$$W^m = 443 + 1.57WPT^m.$$

Table 2–3, reveals that the average male employee has 195 total points and earns a monthly salary of $750, while the average female has 240 points and earns $656. If women were paid according to the male scale, then the above equation predicts that the average woman would earn:

$$\overline{W} = 443 + 1.57(240.5) = \$821$$

which would amount to about a 20 percent pay increase. To one supporter at least the conclusion is obvious:

[we are paying] one class of employees (women) at a lower rate of pay in order to maintain another group of employees (men) at an artificially high one (Remick n. d.:64).

LOONEY TUNES?

Critics of comparable worth usually hoot at the idea that jobs can be "valued" in any objective sense. William Niskanan, while on President Reagan's Council of Economic Advisors, called it a "truly crazy idea" (*National Review* 1984:17). To Clarence Pendleton, Reagan-appointed chairman of the U.S. Civil Rights Commission, it is the "looniest idea since 'Looney Tunes'" (*Daily Labor Report* 223, Nov. 19, 1984:A–2). And according to Charles Krauthammer (1984:17) of the *New Republic,*

Table 2–2. Regressions of Earnings on Job Worth Points: Coefficients (and t-statistics).

	Washington State (Minimum Monthly Salary, 1976)			
	Male Jobs		Female Jobs	
Equation number	1	2	3	4
Variables				
C	443(14.2)	447(8.9)	353(16.1)	370(15.8)
WPT	1.57(10.4)	—	1.26(15.1)	—
WP4	—	1.29(0.4)	—	−2.37(1.2)
WP5	—	1.57(9.8)	—	1.25(15.4)
R^2	.662	.662	.804	.815
N	63	63	58	58

	Minnesota (Maximum Monthly Salary, 1983)			
	Male Jobs		Female Jobs	
Equation number	5	6	7	8
Variables				
C	1012(40.7)	1009(17.8)	733(36.2)	729(33.9)
HPT	3.27(25.3)	—	3.50(33.8)	—
HP4	—	3.46(1.1)	—	4.76(02.0)
HP5	—	3.28(21.1)	—	3.51(33.1)
R^2	.865	.865	.962	.963
N	102	102	48	48

Source: Ehrenberg and Smith (1984) Tables 4 and 7. For definitions and means of variables, see Table 2–3 below.

it is, above all, a mandate for arbitrariness: every subjective determination, no matter how whimsically arrived at, is first enshrined in a number to give it an entirely specious solidity, then added to another number no less insubstantial, to yield a total entirely meaningless.

These and other critics have essentially levied three charges against the use of job evaluation to measure the "worth" of different jobs: (1) its subjectivity and arbitrariness, (2) its failure to

Table 2–3. Mean Values and Definitions of Variables Employed in Job Worth Regressions.

	Washington State			*Minnesota*	
Variable	*Male Jobs*	*Female Jobs*	*Variable*	*Male Jobs*	*Female Jobs*
Wage	$750	$656	Wage	$1944	$1364
WPT	195.2	240.5	HPT	285.7	180.5
WP4	8.7	4.4	HP4	5.4	1.4
WP5	186.5	236.1	HP5	280.3	179.1

WAGE = monthly salary (Washington State 1976; Minnesota, 1983)
WPT = knowledge and skill + mental demands + accountability + working conditions
WP4 = working conditions
WP5 = *WPT* − *WP4*
HPT = know-how + problem solving + accountability + working conditions
HP4 = working conditions
HP5 = *HPT* − *HP4*

Source: Ehrenberg and Smith (1984) Tables 3 and 6 and calculations by the authors.

capture all of the relevant determinants of job wages, and (3) its failure to incorporate the demand side of the market. We review and evaluate several issues related to these charges below.

The Subjectivity of Job Evaluation

Advocates of comparable worth appear to agree that all present job evaluation systems reflect cultural values and, presumably, biases. The National Academy of Sciences' review of job evaluation categorically states that "job evaluation inherently rests on subjective judgements" (Treiman 1979:39), while Steinberg and Haignere (1984:17) describe the procedure as a way of "systematizing value systems." But they seem to believe that although values cannot be removed, biases can be. Thus, at one point Helen Remick asserts that "The search for a bias free system does not imply the search for a value free one." She goes on to state that

we can reasonably seek the equitable application of already existing cultural values and the alteration only of those which are obviously biased (Remick 1983:1671).

But how is it possible to construct a system that is both bias free and yet reflects cultural values? Whose cultural values are the "biased" ones that are to be purged, Winn Newman's or William Niskanen's? Is weighting "accountability" up to 2,800 points and working conditions up to 66 a cultural value or a bias? Job evaluation is a way of expressing *somebody's* values. Surely the critics are right on this much: Job evaluation is subjective, and job ratings will very likely seem arbitrary to anyone who does not share the evaluators' values.

Arbitrariness of the Factor Weights

While advocates seem to believe that present job evaluation systems are prone to be sex-biased, comparable worth job evaluations appear to be weighted against blue-collar jobs and manual labor. A glance at the Willis scales in Table 2–1 reveals that working conditions receive less than one-tenth of the weight implicitly attached to "knowledge" by the scales. Given that job evaluation systems are often designed and implemented by professionals, these weights might not seem surprising. Moreover, working conditions tend to be either negatively correlated with or independent of other factors (Ehrenberg and Smith 1984). This fact, plus the low weight that they receive, ensures that jobs that score high on "knowledge" or similar factors receive a large number of total points, while jobs that score high on working conditions will typically receive relatively few points. Thus we see in Table 2–1 that while laundry workers score twice as high as registered nurses in working conditions, their jobs receive less than one-fifth the total Willis points.

In fact the Hay and Willis schemes mirror the market (and for that matter the occupational status indexes) in their low evaluation of blue-collar jobs. There is little empirical evidence of compensating wage differentials for strenuous and unpleasant working conditions, especially in female-dominated jobs such as laundry workers. Nevertheless, for whatever cultural or institutional reasons (such as, trade unions), there are many male-dominated, blue-collar jobs that pay quite well relative to female-dominated jobs that are ostensibly more intellectually demanding. Thus, it is probably no accident that comparable worth advocates are fond of comparing earnings in female-dominated

Table 2–4. Why Don't These Women Earn More?

Jobs	Sex Domination	Monthly Salary	Job Evaluation Points
Librarian I	F	$ 750	288
Street sweeper operator	M	758	124
Senior accounting clerk	F	1,343	169
Baker	M	1,343	147
Senior library clerk	F	614	178
Water-meter reader	M	630	98
Executive secretary	F	1,423	199
Senior groundskeeper	M	1,423	167

Source: United States Congress, House, Committee on Post Office and Civil Service (1983): 968.

white-collar jobs with male-dominated blue-collar jobs, as has been done in Table 2–4.

Some idea of how the weighting scheme can determine who is and who is not found to be underpaid can be gleaned from the following example. In Washington state the average man's job scored 195 total points, while the average woman's job received 240 points (Table 2–3). That this result depends crucially on the weighting scheme can be demonstrated by arbitrarily multiplying each of the first three factors (summed in the variable WP5) by .5 and the fourth (WP4) by 10. This will not change the relative rank of men and women on any given factor but will simply weight them differently, giving relatively more weight to "working conditions" in the total. If this is done, women now average 162 points and men about 186 points, and presto, men's jobs really are "worth" more. Admittedly, this reweighting of factors is entirely arbitrary and "biases" the evaluation in favor of blue-collar men's jobs. But is it any more arbitrary or biased than Willis's weighting? Perhaps, but many blue-collar workers might not agree.

Moreover, although some comparable worth advocates have claimed that it would benefit minorities (Comparable Worth

Table 2–5. Effect of Alternative Weighting Systems on Job Evaluation Scores by Race and Sex.

Factor	Weighting Systems								
	1	2	3	4	5	6	7	8	9
Data	1	10	1	1	1	1	1	1	1
People	1	1	10	1	1	1	10	1	1
Things	1	1	1	10	1	1	1	1	10
Strength	1	1	1	1	10	1	1	10	10
Environment	1	1	1	1	1	10	1	10	10

Alternative Scales and Job Evaluation Scores by Race and Sex

	White Males	White Females	Black Males	Black Females
Scale 1	8.3	6.9	8.3	6.7
Scale 2	28.3	24.6	24.3	20.8
Scale 3	21.7	19.8	19.4	17.7
Scale 4	21.0	20.1	22.1	18.6
Scale 5	30.5	23.6	34.2	26.4
Scale 6	14.4	8.9	16.5	9.8
Scale 7	41.6	37.4	35.2	31.9
Scale 8	36.6	25.5	42.4	29.6
Scale 9	49.3	38.7	56.2	41.5

Source: Treiman (1984): (Tables 3 and 5).

Project 1985), there is reason to believe that schemes that attach low weights to working conditions may place blacks at the bottom of the rating system. Calculations by Donald Treiman (1984) show how this could work. Treiman weighted five "factors" used by the Dictionary of Occupational Titles—data, people, things, strength, and environment—by nine different weighting systems. The weighting systems and their impact on mean point scores by sex and race are presented in Table 2–5.

As Treiman notes, none of these scales results in higher values for women's than men's jobs, but important differences do emerge. Black women are always on the bottom unless scale 5 is employed. Scale 3 places all blacks on the bottom, while scales 8 and 9 place black men on the top. Moreover, in data not reproduced here, Treiman has also shown that if scores are broken down by manual and nonmanual occupations, scales 2, 3, and 7 would place white women in nonmanual jobs above white men in manual jobs, while the other scales would reverse this result. And not surprisingly, the scales that would put women in nonmanual occupations on top would put women in manual occupations on the bottom. Thus, depending on how job factors are weighted, the implementation of comparable worth could indeed improve the relative position of white women in white-collar jobs, but perhaps at the expense of black workers and workers in blue-collar jobs. We return to this subject in Chapter 5 where we estimate the impact of comparable worth on different occupational and demographic groups.

Ambiguity of the Wage Equations

While the weights attached to the factors in a job evaluation are one source of its arbitrariness, the scales employed are another. And this type of arbitrariness makes the entire enterprise of translating job points into wage rates problematic. To see this, consider the following two equations for men's and women's jobs taken from columns 5 and 7 in Table 2–2:

$$W^m = 1012 + 3.27 HPT^m; \quad \overline{W}^m = \$1946; \quad \overline{HPT}^m = 286 \qquad \text{(Eq. 2.1)}$$
$$W^f = 733 + 3.50\ HPT^f; \quad \overline{W}^f = \$1364; \quad \overline{HPT}^f = 181 \qquad \text{(Eq. 2.2)}$$

Taken literally, equations (2.1) and (2.2) imply that each Hay point raises wages in male jobs by \$3.27 per month and wages in female jobs by \$3.50 per month! Women are thus *overcompensated* for their Hay points relative to men, and for men's and women's jobs with the same number of points the entire wage gap (and more) is due to the difference between the constant terms of the equations.[3]

As described in Appendix 2–C, this wage gap can be partitioned as follows:

$$\overline{W}^m - \overline{W}^f = (1012 - 732) + \overline{HPT}^f (3.27 - 3.50) + 3.50(\overline{HPT}^m - \overline{HPT}^f)$$

$$\text{(Eq. 2.3)}$$

Plugging the mean level of Hay points for male and female jobs into equation (2.3) partitions the $582 per month salary gap as follows:

$280 due to differences in constants;
$368 due to differences in mean level of Hay points;
−$66 due to differences in coefficients.

Thus, in this particular application we would *reduce* earnings in women's jobs by $66 per month if we substituted the male job coefficient for the female job coefficient. This is not likely to advance the cause of pay equity.

If comparable worth were to use the male job equation to set wages in all jobs, it would raise the pay in most women's jobs, but it would do so entirely because the male equation has a larger constant term. In fact, it would do so *despite* the fact that male jobs actually pay a lower return to HPT! But this constant term represents what we don't know (that is, what the job point variable in our wage equation doesn't explain) about the level of wages for a given level of job points. To claim that this procedure corrects for discrimination implicitly assumes that all economically relevant (and thus presumably justifiable) determinants of male/female wage differences are accounted for by differences in levels of HPT. This is obviously not the case for Willis or Hay evaluations or any other job rating system.

Most likely a substantial portion of the difference in these constant term *is* due to discrimination in setting the pay for women's jobs, but there is no way of knowing how much. We could simply assume that *all* of the difference in constants is discrimination, which may please comparable worth advocates but certainly not skeptics. Or we may assume that *none* of it is (thus, only equating coefficients but not constants), which may satisfy conservatives but certainly not advocates. To the extent that the explanatory variables in the wage equations fail to capture all of the economically relevant determinants of wages, the first approach will overstate the role of discrimination in the male/female wage gap, and the second approach will understate it.

As we show in Appendix 2–C, the problem here involves more than the fact that our earnings equations omit important determinants of earnings. Due to the fundamental arbitrariness of the job trait scales (which presumably have no natural or unique origin in the same sense that zero years of work experience means no work experience), it is not possible unambiguously to partition the wage gap into a portion due to differences in coefficients and a portion due to differences in constants. Suppose, for example, that we add 100 points to the mean Hay points of both men's and women's jobs. The regression equations and means will now be

$$W^m = 703 + 3.27 HPT^m; \overline{HPT}^m = 386 \qquad \text{(Eq. 2.4)}$$
$$W^f = 382 + 3.50 HPT^f; \overline{HPT}^f = 281 \qquad \text{(Eq. 2.5)}$$

The difference in constant terms now becomes $321 (an increase of $41). The portion of the wage gap due to levels of HPT remains the same. But the portion due to differences in coefficients becomes −$107 (a decline of $41). The change in job point scales would not affect our wage adjustments if we used both the coefficient and the constant term of the male equation to adjust women's wages, but it would affect the indicated wage adjustments if we adjusted only for differences in men's and women's coefficients (with female-dominated jobs retaining their own constant term).

Thus, it seems to us that the arbitrary scales employed in current job evaluation studies largely vitiate their results. If one simply uses the male job equation to set wages in women's jobs, the result is surely to "correct" for more than discrimination. This may not bother comparable worth advocates, but it is not what they say they are doing. Some practitioners seem aware of this problem, defining comparable worth to require equal *returns* to (that is, coefficients on) job traits.[4] But as we have shown here and elaborated in Appendix 2–C, this "correction" can be arbitrarily raised or lowered simply by changing the scale on which the factors are measured.

The Role of Supply and Demand

Even if jobs' compensable factors were measured uniquely and accurately, changes in demand for a particular kind of skill or knowledge can result in sharp short-run differences in job earnings and in returns to compensable factors. As critics rhetorically ask: Should college Spanish teachers receive the same pay as petroleum engineers even if the jobs are thought to require equal levels of "skill"? (Bunzel 1982). While this objection points to the need for some flexibility in the use of job evaluations to set pay rates, it probably has little to do with persistent earnings differences between nurses and tree trimmers or secretaries and garbage collectors (Remick 1984). Such persistent differentials, we suspect, are more likely to result from discrimination, employer cartels, differential bargaining power, or unmeasured job characteristics that reflect the more desirable aspects of white-collar compared to blue-collar jobs (Killingsworth 1984).

CONCLUSION

Our review of the legal status of comparable worth suggests that politically it is an idea whose time seems to have come—at least for the public sector. An increasing number of cities and states have undertaken job evaluations—often spurred on by union demands and the threat of lawsuits—and women's groups and unions such as AFSCME are pressing for legislation in a number of states. As history has shown, the states have often taken the lead in protective legislation that eventually was adopted at the federal level. Although the Supreme Court opened the door to comparable worth in *Gunther*, it seems unlikely to swing wide the portals any time soon. Comparable worth seems more likely to come through piecemeal legislation on the state and local level and through collective bargaining than be mandated by the federal courts.

We conclude that comparable worth job evaluations as presently undertaken fail to identify and correct for that part of the male/female wage gap that can be unambiguously attributed to discrimination in general or the devaluation of "women's jobs." Weightings are inherently subjective, and alternative weightings produce different rankings among job classes and groups of workers. In addition, any procedure that automatically equates the constant terms in men's and women's equations is open to the serious objection that it is correcting for more than sex discrimination. Yet if one attempts to correct only for differences in returns to job factors, the resulting adjustment will be an artifact of the scales on which job worth is measured and thus no less arbitrary than the scales themselves.

Yet comparable worth wage corrections need not be this arbitrary. More complete measures of job characteristics can be developed, and variables that have unique, nonarbitrary scales and more objectively determined weights employed. And approaches that specifically isolate wage differences due to discrimination against workers in women's jobs can be developed. We will turn to this task in Chapter 4.

APPENDIX 2–A
STATE COMPARABLE WORTH ACTIVITIES

State	Activity[a]
Alaska	Added CW language to its FEP law (1980). A job-evaluation study undertaken in 1984. Public health nurses case is before state Human Rights Commission.
Arkansas	A 1955 statute covering state workers prohibits wage discrimination for "comparable work" but allows "reasonable differentiations."
California	A 1981 law mandates CW for state workers; a 1983 law prohibits local laws that preclude consideration of CW; a 1983 law added CW language to FEP law. A task force is studying public and private pay inequity and the State Employees Association filed a Title VII action in federal court in 1984.
Connecticut	Job evaluation (Willis) of state employment (1979); CW is being implemented by collective bargaining. AFSCME negotiated pay equity raise for clerical workers in 1983 and has funded a comparable worth suit for state clerical employees in federal court.
Delaware	A 1983 state law mandates CW for state workers.

APPENDIX 2–A *continued*

State	Activity[a]
Florida	CW legislation is being drafted (1984).
Georgia	A 1966 law mandates CW for state workers.
Hawaii	A 1981 resolution urges CW on private employers; a 1982 law requires report and recommendations on CW for state workers. Hawaii Government Employees and AFSCME filed Title VII suit in federal court in 1984.
Idaho	A 1969 law mandates CW for state workers; a 1977 law requires JE for state workers.
Illinois	A 1982 law appropriated $10,000 for pilot JE study of civil service; language adding CW to EPA pending of 1984. AFSCME won pay equity raise for state word processors in 1983. Illinois Nurses Association filed comparable worth suit in Federal Court in 1984.
Indiana	A 1984 law appropriated funds to study CW.
Iowa	A 1983 law appropriated $150,000 for JE study of civil service and established CW for state workers. In fiscal 1983, $10 million appropriated for implementation.
Kansas	CW JE study underway in 1984.
Kentucky	A 1966 law mandates CW for state workers; 1982 law appropriated $14,000 for JE study.
Louisiana	JE study underway in 1984.
Maine	CW JE study underway in 1984; 1954 law mandates CW for state workers.
Maryland	A 1966 law mandates CW for state workers; CW JE is underway. Governor has requested a special 7 percent raise for female-dominated clerical jobs.

APPENDIX 2–A *continued*

State	Activity[a]
Massachusetts	A 1945 law mandates CW for state workers; a 1983 law appropriated $75,000 for JE study of civil service.
Michigan	A 1962 law mandates CW for state workers; a CW study has been completed. State Employees Association filed comparable worth suit in federal court in 1984.
Minnesota	A 1982 law establishes CW policy and process for civil service; a 1983 law appropriated $21.7 million for CW wage increases; a 1984 law requires CW for localities. Librarians at the University of Minnesota won nearly $1 million in pre-trial CW settlement.
Missouri	A 1983 law established CW as state policy; a CW study is underway.
Montana	A CW JE study was required by 1983 law.
Nebraska	A CW JE study was required by 1978 law.
Nevada	A 1983 law required preliminary study of civil service.
New Hampshire	A CW JE study is underway.
New Jersey	A 1984 law established task force and appropriated $300,000 to study civil service.
New Mexico	A CW JE study underway in 1984; in 1983, $3.3 million appropriated to raise pay of lowest-paid workers.
New York	A CW JE study, funded with $750,000, is underway.
North Carolina	A 1984 law authorized $650,000 to study pay equity for state workers.
North Dakota	A CW JE study was completed; EPA has CW language.
Ohio	A 1965 law mandates CW for state employees; a CW JE study underway in 1984.

APPENDIX 2–A *continued*

State	Activity[a]
Ohio	A commission is studying state pay system: 1985–86 budget contains $9 million to phase in pay equity.
Oregon	A 1983 law appropriated $300,00 for CW JE study of civil service.
Pennsylvania	A CW JE study was completed; legislation to add CW language to EPA law pending.
Rhode Island	A CW JE study underway in 1984.
South Dakota	A 1966 law mandates CW for state workers; March 1985 law authorizes study to classify jobs and appropriates funds for raises.
Tennessee	A CW JE study underway in 1984.
Vermont	A CW JE study was completed.
Virginia	A 1984 law requires research on CW.
Washington	A 1977 law requires biennial update of 1974 JE study; 1983 law sets up ten-year plan to implement CW for civil service, $1.5 million appropriated to raise wages of lowest-paid workers.
West Virginia	A CW JE study underway in 1984. EPA contains CW language.
Wisconsin	A 1977 law mandates CW for state workers. Legislation in 1984 appropriated $300,000 for CW study.

a. CW is comparable worth; JE is job evaluation; EPA is employment practices act; FEP is fair employment practices.

Source: Ehrenberg and Smith (1984: Table 1); Cook (1983); Chi (1984: Table 3); Rothchild (1984: Appendix); *Comparable Worth Project Newsletter* (various issues); Equal Employment Advisory Council (1985); Bureau of National Affairs (1981, 1985a).

APPENDIX 2–B
COMPARABLE WORTH ON THE LOCAL LEVEL
(a selected listing)

State	Activity[a]
Arizona	
Phoenix	A JE study; wage adjustments contemplated or implemented.
Tucson s. d.	A JE study
California	
Alameda Co.	Information gathering
Belmont	AFSCME negotiated pay increases
Berkeley	Information gathering
Chico s. d.	JE study; wage adjustments contemplated
Contra Costa Co.	JE study
Fresno	JE study
Humboldt Co.	JE study; wage adjustments contemplated
Long Beach	Implementation
Los Angeles	AFSCME negotiated pay increases; JE for school district
Los Gatos	Pay equity policy
Mountain View	JE study
Palo Alto	CW litigation
Sacramento s. d.	JE study negotiated by SEIU
Sonoma Co.	JE study
San Jose	JE study; AFSCME negotiated pay increases
San Lorenzo s. d.	JE study
San Francisco	JE study
San Mateo ca.	AFSCME negotiated pay increases
Santa Clara Co.	JE study; SEIU negotiated pay adjustments
Santa Cruz	JE study; wage adjustments contemplated
Colorado	
Colorado Springs	JE study
Maryland	
Montgomery Co. s. d.	Information gathering

APPENDIX 2–B *continued*

State	Activity[a]
Minnesota	
Anoka Co.	CW litigation
Minneapolis	JE study
Minnetonka s. d.	Negotiated CW wage increases
Northfield s. d.	Information gathering
Osseo s. d.	Information gathering
Princeton	JE study and implementation
St. Paul	JE study
New York	
Nassau	JE study; CW litigation
New York City	CW litigation
Oregon	
Portland	JE study
Pennsylvania	
Philadelphia	CW litigation
Pittsburgh s. d.	SEIU negotiated pay increases
Vermont	
Burlington	CW implementation
Virginia	
Virginia Beach	JE study
Fairfax Co.	CW litigation
Washington	
Bellevue	JE study and implementation
King Co.	CW wage increases to be implemented
Olympia	JE study
Renton	JE study
Seattle	JE study
Spokane	JE study; AFSCME negotiated pay increases for female-dominated jobs
Wisconsin	
Madison	JE study

a. CW is comparable worth; JE is job evaluation.
Source: Ehrenberg and Smith (1984: Table 1); Chi (1984: Table 3); Rothchild (1984: Appendix); *Comparable Worth Project Newsletter* (various issues); Equal Employment Advisory Council (1985); Bureau of National Affairs (1981, 1985a).

APPENDIX 2–C
PARTITIONING THE WAGE GAP

Suppose we have two simple regressions of men's and women's wages as a function of a single "job trait" variable, T. Since the regression line passes through the means of all the variables in the equation, it holds that

$$\overline{W}^m = a^m + b^m\overline{T}^m$$

and

$$\overline{W}^f = a^f + b^f\overline{T}^f$$

Subtracting the female from the male equation yields

$$\overline{W}^m - \overline{W}^f = a^m - a^f + b^m(\overline{T}^m - \overline{T}^f) + \overline{T}^f(b^m - b^f)$$

Here, the wage gap is partitioned into (1) a part due to differences in constant terms, (2) a part due to differences in mean levels of the independent variable(s), and (3) a part due to differences in the coefficients of (or returns to) the independent variable(s). In this case we have followed the usual procedure of evaluating the difference in levels of T at the male "return" and differences in returns at the mean female level of T. But we could just as well have subtracted the male equation from the female, thus reversing all the superscripts in the above equation. The choice of a reference equation is logically arbitrary (though it will yield different results). The male equation is usually chosen as the reference, based on the premise that the male wage structure is the nondiscriminatory norm.

Problems arise with this procedure, however, when variables with arbitrary scales (such as Hay points, DOT job measures, or factor scores) are used to explain wage differences between groups of workers (or jobs). As Jones (1983) has shown and as we have argued in this chapter, it is not possible in this case uniquely to determine the portion of the wage gap due to differences in constants versus the portion due to differences in coefficients.

For example, consider the following hypothetical data on wages and job trait T:

W^m	T^m	W^f	T^f
$20	0	$10	0
40	1	20	1
60	2	30	2
80	3	40	3
100	4	50	4

Now $\overline{W}^m = \$60$, $\overline{W}^f = \$30$, and $\overline{T}^m = \overline{T}^f = 2$. These data exactly fit the following equations:

$$W^m = 20 + 20T^m \text{ and } W^f = 10 + 10T^f$$

and partitioning the male/female wage gap yields the following result:

$$\overline{W}^m - \overline{W}^f = (20 - 10) + 20(2 - 2) + 2(20 - 10)$$

$$\begin{array}{ccc} \text{due to} & \text{due to} & \text{due to} \\ \text{different} & \text{different} & \text{different} \\ \text{constants} & \text{levels of } T & \text{coefficients} \end{array}$$

Of the total wage gap of $30, $10 appears to be due to the difference in constant terms and $20 due to the difference in co-efficients of T. But now suppose that T is measured on a scale running from 1 to 5 rather than from 0 to 4. This changes the mean of T from 2 to 3, and the equations to

$$W^m = 0 + 20T^m \text{ and } W^f = 0 + 10T^f$$

Partitioning the wage gap now yields

$$\overline{W}^m - \overline{W}^f = (0 - 0) + 20(3 - 3) + 3(20 - 10)$$

Now *all* of the wage gap is attributed to differences in the coefficients of T. More generally, we conclude that when arbitrarily scaled variables are used in the wage equation, the contribution to the wage gap of differences in the *levels* of those variables can be uniquely calculated. But the remaining gap cannot be uniquely or unambiguously partitioned into a portion due to differences in coefficients and a portion due to differences in constant terms.

NOTES

1. Disparate impact refers to facially neutral employment practices that have an adverse effect on a protected group. Under the disparate impact doctrine (established in *Griggs v. Duke Power Co.*, 401 U.S. 424 (1971)) no intent to discriminate, but only a discriminatory effect, need be shown.
2. This development has put the job evaluation consultants, such as Hay and Willis, in an awkward position. The comparable worth movement has created a boom for the job evaluation industry, but the downside is that it may make employers more reluctant to voluntarily undertake job evaluations. In its public statements on the role of job evaluation in comparable worth Hay Associates (Bellak, Bates, and Glasner 1983) expresses strong agreement on every side of the question. Thus, on one hand, "job evaluation is clearly a friend of comparable worth. . . . it frequently shows that lower level female dominated jobs are paid less per unit of content than lower level male dominated jobs" (p. 423). But on the other hand, "Job evaluation will not provide a foundation with such broad acceptance and demonstrable validity to support the changes that the advocates of comparable worth seek. In our opinion, the key to ending systematic pay discrimination is already at hand under equal opportunity laws" (p. 424). Finally, however, we are assured that, "For us at Hay Associates, whatever comparable worth issues we see . . . recognizing the issues does not mean we walk away from them" (Bellak 1984:81).
3. This result is not an isolated statistical fluke. In a study by Treiman, Hartmann, and Roos (1984:Table 9–2) coefficients on 5 of the 6 explanatory variables were higher for the sample of female-dominated occupations than for the sample of male-dominated occupations. The authors seem unfazed by this result and do not discuss it in their paper. Likewise, the female-dominated jobs in our sample (introduced in Chapter 3) yield higher "returns" (coefficients) to schooling, work experience, and job tenure than do the male-dominated jobs.
4. The premise of most comparable worth studies is that "jobs with equal points are assumed to merit equal pay" (Remick n.d.:50). In terms of our wage equations this implies that women should be given both the constant terms and coefficients from male or all jobs. And in fact, Remick (n.d.) computes women's "expected" salary by employing an equation for all workers. In constrast, Hartmann and Treiman (1983:413) give an equation defining "job worth" as equal to job factor scores times job factor weights, where the weights are coefficients of job factor scores in a regression of job wages on job scores. This procedure presumably does *not* equate constant terms but only coefficients. In the same vein, Treiman, Hartmann, and Roos (1984) state that comparable worth rejects "different returns to such pay-related factor as years of schooling, years of experience, complexity of the job" and proposes "to reward women's jobs in the same way as men's jobs—that is, to give women's jobs the same returns on such factors as men's jobs" (pp. 137–38). But what they actually do is to give women's jobs both the male coefficients *and constant term*. In conclusion, they return to their original definition, interpreting their results as showing that "the bulk of the earnings gap is due to difference in the rate of return on characteristics" (p. 148). Finally, David Pierson, Karen Koziara, and Russell Johannesson (1983) employ factor scores from a factor analysis of job content data to measure job content and, like Remick, compute the impact on the wage gap of giving women the men's constant term and regression coefficients.

BIBLIOGRAPHY

Beatty, Richard, and James R. Beatty. 1984. "Some Problems with Contemporary Job Evaluation Systems." In *Comparable Worth and Wage Discrimination*, edited by Helen Remick, pp. 59–78. Philadelphia: Temple University Press.

Bellak, Alvin O. 1984. "Comparable Worth: A Practitioner's View." In *Comparable Worth: Issue for the 80's*, Vol. 1, pp. 75–82. Washington, D.C.: U.S. Commission of Civil Rights Hearings.

Bellak, A.; M. Bates; and D. Glasner. 1983. "Job Evaluation: Its Role in the Comparable Worth Debate." In *Public Personnel Management* 12 (Winter):418–24.

Bittman, Mark, and Bob Arnold. 1984. "Comparable Worth is Put to the Test at Yale." *Business Week* (Nov. 26):92 + .

Bunzel, John. 1982. "To Each According to Her Worth?" *Public Interest* 67 (Spring):77–93.

Bureau of National Affairs. 1981. *The Comparable Worth Issue: A BNA Special Report*. Washington, D.C.

Business Week. 1979. "The New Pay Push for Women." (Dec. 17):66 + .

———. ." (Nov.26):92 + .

Chi, Keon. 1984. "Comparable Worth: Implications of the Washington Case." *State Government* 57, no. 2:34–45.

Comparable Worth Project. 1982–1985. *Newsletter*. Oakland, Calif.

Cook, Alice. 1983. *Comparable Worth: The Problem and States' Approaches to Wage Equity*. Manoa, Hawaii: University of Hawaii at Manoa, Industrial Relations Center.

Cowley, Geoffrey. 1984. "Comparable Worth: Another Terrible Idea." *Washington Monthly* 15 (Jan.):52–57.

Daily Labor Report. 1984–1985. Washington, D.C.: Bureau of National Affairs, Inc.

Ehrenberg, Ronald, and Robert Smith. 1984. "Comparable Worth in the Public Sector." *Working Paper* No. 1471. Cambridge, Mass.: National Bureau of Economic Research.

Equal Employment Advisory Council. 1985. "Chart of State Comparable Worth Developments as of February 15, 1985." Washington, D.C.: Equal Employment Advisory Council.

Farnquist, Robert, and Russell Strausbaugh. 1983. "Pandora's Worth: The San Jose Experience." *Public Personnel Management Journal* 12 (Dec.):358–68.

Freeman, Richard, and Jonathan Leonard. 1984. "Union Maids: Unions and the Female Workforce." Paper presented to the Conference on Gender in the Workplace sponsored by the Committee on the Status of Women and Economics and the Brookings Institution, Nov. 15–16.

Friendly, David T. 1985. "This Isn't Shakespeare." *Newsweek* (Mar. 18):62.

Golper, John. 1983. "The Current Legal Status of Comparable Worth in the Federal Courts." *Labor Law Journal* 34 (Sept.):563–80.

Gregory, R. G., and R. C. Duncan. 1981. "Segmented Labor Market Theories and the Australian Experience of Equal Pay for Women." *Journal of Post Keynesian Economics* 3 (Spring):403–29.

Hartmann, Heidi, and Donald Treiman. 1983. "Notes on the NAS Study of Equal Pay for Jobs of Equal Value." *Public Personnel Management Journal* 12 (Winter):404–17.

Heen, Mary. 1984. "A Review of Federal Court Decisions under Title VII of the Civil Rights Act of 1964." In *Comparable Worth and Wage Discrimination*, edited by Helen Remick, pp. 197–219. Philadelphia: Temple University Press.

Hildebrand, George. 1980. "The Market System." In *Comparable Worth: Issues and Alternatives*, edited by E. R. Livernash, pp. 79–106. Washington, D.C.: Equal Employment Advisory Council.

Jones, F. L. 1983. "On Decomposing the Wage Gap: A Critical Comment on Blinder's Method." *Journal of Human Resources* 18 (Winter):126–30.

Killingsworth, Mark. 1984. "A Simple Structural Model of Heterogeneous Preferences and Compensating Wage Differentials." Unpublished paper, Rutgers University.

Krauthammer, Charles. 1984. "From Bad to Worth." *New Republic* (July 30):16–18.

Kurtz, Maxine, and E. Clyde Hocking. 1983. "Nurses v. Tree Trimmers." *Public Personnel Management Journal* 12 (Winter):369–81.

Levin, Michael. 1984. "Comparable Worth: The Feminist Road to Socialism." *Commentary* 78 (Sept.):13–19.

McGuire, Mike. 1982. "A New Way to Equal Pay." *Dollars and Sense* (April):12–14.

National Review. 1984. (Nov.):17.

New York Times. 1982–1985.

Pierson, D.; K. Koziara; and R. Johannesson. 1983. "Equal Pay for Jobs of Comparable Worth: A Quantified Job Content Approach." *Public Personnel Management Journal* 12 (Winter):445–60.

Portman, L.; J. A. Grune; and E. Johnson. 1984. "The Role of Labor." In *Comparable Worth and Wage Discrimination*, edited by Helen Remick, pp. 219–37. Philadelphia: Temple University Press.

Remick, Helen. 1983. "The Comparable Worth Controversy." In Committee on the Post Office and Civil Service, Joint Hearings, *Pay Equity: Equal Pay for Work of Comparable Value* II, 97th Cong. 2d Sess., pp. 1666–86. Washington, D.C.

———. 1984. "Major Issues in *A Priori* Applications." In *Comparable Worth and Wage Discrimination*, edited by Helen Remick, pp. 99–117. Philadelphia: Temple University Press.

———. n.d. "Comparable Worth: Equal Pay for Equal Worth." In *Education Equity Issues in Community Colleges*, pp. 50–66. Pullman, Wash.: Northwest Women Studies Resource Bank, Washington State University.

Rothchild, Nina. 1984."Overview of Pay Initiatives, 1974–1984." In U.S. Civil Rights Commission, *Comparable Worth: Issue for the 80's* 2, pp. 119–30. Washington, D.C.

Schwab, Donald. 1980. "Job Evaluation and Pay Setting: Concepts and Practices." In *Comparable Worth: Issues and Alternatives,* edited by E. R. Livernash, pp. 49–77. Washington, D.C.: Equal Employment Advisory Council.

———. 1984. "Using Job Evaluation to Obtain Pay Equity." U.S. Commission on Civil Rights. *Comparable Worth: Issue for the 80's,* 1, pp. 83–92. Washington, D.C.

Siniscalco, Gary, and Cynthia Remmers. 1984. "Comparable Worth in the Aftermath of *AFSCME v. State of Washington.*" *Employee Relations Law Journal* 10 (Summer):6–29.

Steinberg, Ronnie. 1984. "Statement." In *Comparable Worth: Issue for the 80's,* Vol. 2, pp. 55–72. Washington, D.C.: U.S. Commission of Civil Rights Hearings.

Steinberg, Ronnie, and Lois Haignere. 1984. "Separable but Equivalent: Equal Pay for Work of Comparable Worth." In *Gender at Work,* pp. 13–26. Washington, D.C.: Women's Research and Education Institute.

Thomas, Clarence. 1983. "Pay Equity and Comparable Worth." *Labor Law Journal* 34 (Jan.):3–12.

Treiman, Donald. 1979. *Job Evaluation: An Analytic Review.* Washington, D.C.: National Academy of Sciences.

———. 1984. "Effect of Choice of Factors and Factor Weights in Job Evaluation." In *Comparable Worth and Wage Discrimination,* edited by Helen Remick, pp. 79–98. Philadelphia: Temple University Press.

Treiman, Donald, and Heidi Hartmann, eds. 1981. *Women, Work, and Wages.* Washington, D.C.: National Academy of Sciences.

Treiman, D.; H. Hartmann; and P. Roos. 1984. "Assessing Pay Discrimination Using National Data." In *Comparable Worth and Wage Discrimination,* edited by Helen Remick, pp. 137–54. Philadelphia: Temple University Press.

U.S. Congress, House, Committee on Post Office and Civil Service, Joint Hearings. 1983. *Pay Equity: Equal Pay for Work of Comparable Value.* 97th Cong. 2d Sess., Part II. Washington, D.C.: GPO.

Volz, William J., and Joseph T. Breitenbeck. 1984. "Comparable Worth and the Union's Duty of Fair Representation." *Employee Relations Law Journal* 10 (Summer):30–47.

Wall Street Journal. 1982–1985.

Willis, Norman et al. 1983. "State of Washington Comparable Worth Study." (Sept. 1974) and "Phase II" (Dec. 1976). In U.S. Congress, House Committee on the Post Office and Civil Service, Joint Hearings, *Pay Equity: Equal Pay for Work of Comparable Value* II, 97th Cong., 2d Sess., pp. 1486–596. Washington, D.C.

CHAPTER 3

Sex Discrimination, Occupational Segregation, and Comparable Worth

Dear Abby,
. . . After my sex change, I took a job doing exactly the same work [computer programming] I had done as a man, but as a woman, I am paid $10,000 a year less!
—Taken from the "Dear Abby" column. Copyright, 1985, Universal Press Syndicate. Reprinted with permission. All rights reserved.

No one disputes that there is a pay gap. The dispute is over what causes it.
—LINDA CHAVEZ, staff director of the U.S. Comission on Civil Rights *Daily Labor Report*, Nov. 19, 1984:A2)

INTRODUCTION

This chapter surveys several leading theories of discrimination, develops their implications for occupational segregation, and establishes the importance of occupational segregation in the comparable worth diagnosis of women's low earnings. We then survey and critique existing research measuring the impact of occupational segregation on the male/female earnings gap and present our own estimates of this effect.

LABOR MARKET DISCRIMINATION

The basic theory of wages accepted with varying degrees of reservation by most labor economists may be called a modified human capital model. This theory conceives of both workers and jobs as "bundles of traits" and the labor market as the process by which workers supplying various traits and employers demanding these traits seek each other out and strike a wage bargain. These traits might include (among others) types and levels of education, training, or work experience or tolerance for hazardous or unpleasant working conditions by the worker. Wages of both individuals and jobs will depend on the size and composition of the bundles of traits that each possesses.

WAGE THEORY

To see how wages are set, consider the following example: Suppose a worker is considering how much vocational training to undertake. Additional training has both money costs in the form of tuition and foregone earnings and, perhaps, more or less disutility to the trainee. To employers, training is more or less productive depending on the skill requirements of the jobs they are filling. (A job's skill requirements are usually measured in terms of the amount of time it takes to reach a certain level of proficiency in the job.) Thus, workers will require a wage premium to induce them to undertake more training, and for some jobs employers will be willing to pay such a premium. An efficient labor market will match workers with varying levels of training with jobs requiring various levels of skills, as shown in Figure 3–1 (Becker 1964; Mincer 1962, 1974; Blaug 1976; Ehrenberg and Smith 1982; Hammermesh and Rees 1984).

Figure 3–1 shows how the perfectly competitive labor market determines the increment in earnings a worker receives for each additional year of vocational training. Workers 1 and 2 with given (but different) skills, capacities to absorb training, and "tastes" for training will be indifferent between various combinations of wages and training levels represented by "indifference curves" 1 and 2, respectively. The slope of these curves indicates that workers have to be compensated with higher wages for "investing" in more training. Each worker actually has a whole family of indifference curves and maximizes his or her utility by being on the upper leftmost curve (because movement in the northwest direction represents higher wages and less training).

Likewise, profit-maximizing employers have, given the available technological alternatives, some choice about how they design jobs. The tradeoff between wages and skill requirements in two different jobs (A and B) is represented by the "iso-profit

Figure 3–1. Matching Jobs and Workers.

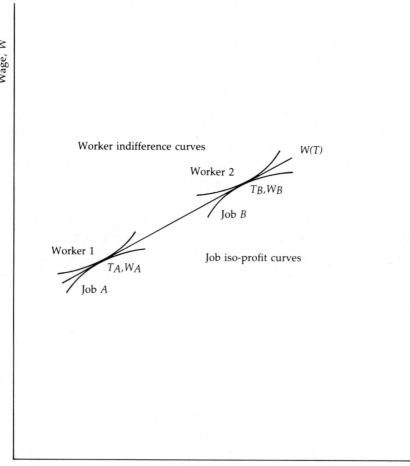

curves" *A* and *B* in Figure 3–1. The slope of these curves indicates that job *A* or job *B* can produce a given level of profit with differing combinations of worker skills (acquired in training) and other inputs (say machines). For example, a grocery market can employ trained cashiers to operate inexpensive cash registers at its checkout counters, or it can use more expensive optical scanners that can be operated by less skilled (cheaper) workers. In other words, it can produce the same result at the same profit using different combinations of physical and human capital.

Each job has whole family of iso-profit curves, and the employer maximize profits by being on the lower rightmost curve (because movement in the southeast direction represents lower wages and more productive workers).

An efficient labor market will match workers to jobs at wage and training levels represented by the tangency points T_A, W_A and T_B, W_B. All such pairings of workers and jobs trace out $W(T)$ —an "envelope" of market clearing, equilibrium transactions between workers and employers that represents the payoff or returns to training for workers.

In a competitive, nondiscriminating labor market in which workers are free to seek out the highest returns that they can make on their training and in which training is the sole determinant of a worker's productivity and earnings, all jobs will pay the same marginal returns to a given level of training, and differences in wages could only be due to differences in *levels* of training.[1] Since much larger earnings differences exist between men and women and between blacks and whites than can be explained by differences in their training or other productive attributes, labor economists have sought to explain these earnings differences by means of several different theories of discrimination (Blau and Jusenius 1976; Reich 1981; Treiman and Hartmann 1981).

THEORIES OF DISCRIMINATION AND OCCUPATIONAL SEGREGATION

Modern efforts to incorporate discrimination into economic theory date from the work of Gary Becker (1957), who simply assumed that employers have a "taste" for discrimination. Applying this model to women implies that the "cost" of hiring a woman equals the wage *plus* the disutility of having her on the payroll. This disutility d can be measured as the decrease in women's wages that would be necessary in order to make the employer indifferent between an equally qualified man and woman.

Suppose for the moment that each employer has the same d value for all jobs but that employers differ among themselves in the size of this value. For some, who don't discriminate, it is zero, and for discriminating employers it ranges from small to large. Figure 3–2 below presents a demand curve, D_1 (or, for the cognoscenti, a marginal productivity schedule) for labor in a given job. Because men and women are assumed to have identical levels of human capital, this schedule is independent of workers' gender. S_f represents the supply of female labor. Suppose that W^m is the wage paid men. If women are also to receive a wage equal to W^m in this job, there must be enough nondiscriminating employers to hire the entire supply of female labor that would be available at this wage. If, at this wage, there is an excess supply of female labor (women are in excess because they are the last hired), then W^f will be less than W^m, and the size of the gap will depend on the amount of excess supply and the size of employers' d values.

Figure 3–2. Employers' Taste for Discrimination and Women's Earnings.

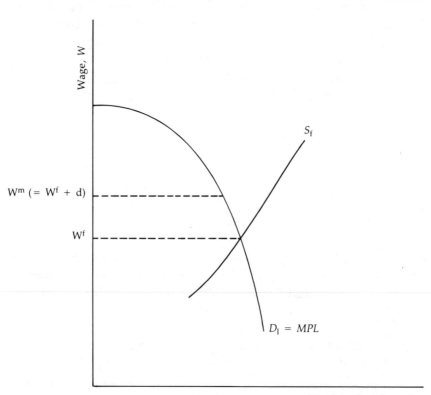

This model is both a theory of wage discrimination and a theory of firm segregation. Employers whose d values exceed $W^m - W^f$ will hire only men; those whose d values are less than $W^m - W^f$ will hire only women. Moreover, since women are paid less than men for identical work, those who hire women have lower costs than those who do not. In a competitive market, they should drive down prices, expand, and eventually drive discriminating employers out of business.

Becker's model becomes a theory of occupational segregation if we now assume that each employer has a different d value for differing jobs (occupations) and that (because prejudice is a social phenomenon) employers are likely to be similar in their rankings of jobs by d values. Moreover, it is likely that pervasive stereotypes about the proper role of women would lead employers to discriminate against women in jobs that place them in positions of authority over men and perhaps in favor of women in subordinate positions or in jobs that mirror women's traditional roles in the home (England 1984; Shepela and Viviano 1984). In such a situation, women will be most prevalent in jobs where employers have zero or low d values, and their wages will be closest to men's in these jobs.

This modified discrimination model suggests that the male/female earnings gap depends on the occupational distribution of men and women and that male/female differences in the occupational distribution are likely to be disadvantageous to women. It also implies that women's earnings levels within occupations are likely to be lower than men's and that the fewer women there are relative to men in the occupation the lower their relative earnings are likely to be. For example, we note that 81 percent of the elementary school teachers in our sample (described below) are women, and they are paid 80 percent of what male elementary school teachers are paid. In contrast, only 9.5 percent of the foremen are women, and they are paid only 60 percent of what male foremen are paid. Finally, this model suggests that if women are restricted from jobs requiring skill, judgment, and the exercise of authority, then their returns to education, training, and experience are also likely to be below men's.

A model that is similar to that of Becker has been proposed by Bergmann (1971). She argues that discrimination works by excluding certain groups of workers from the desirable jobs and crowding them into relatively undesirable jobs. In the case of sex discrimination, this crowding raises the wages of the workers in "male" jobs who are protected from competition and depresses wages in "female" jobs. Bergmann's model does not try to explain occupational segregation but rather *assumes* it and examines the consequences of the occupational crowding that results. Both models assume competitive product markets and, with the exception of the barriers to mobility created by discriminating employers, competitive labor markets. Both therefore imply that unless all employers have the same *d* values, discriminating employers will be driven out of business by non- (or less) discriminating employers that can produce the same product at a lower cost. They thus both have the peculiar property of predicting the long-run nonexistence of the phenomenon they seek to explain.

This result has led some economists to drop the assumption that employers and employees act as "price takers" in the labor market. In fact, there is plenty of evidence of both monopoly and monopsony power in labor markets. For example, a craft union may monopolize the supply of labor in a particular trade. If male craft union members refuse to apprentice or work with women, and have the power to enforce their wills on employers, they can restrict the supply of labor and raise earnings in the monopolized trades. The excluded women will then crowd into other occupations, thereby lowering wages in those jobs. If as a result, women are crowded into low-skill, "dead-end" jobs, their returns to education, training, and experience will be reduced, as well as their wage level. Thus, a monopoly model makes predictions that are virtually identical to those of Becker or Bergmann, with the important exception that in this case, discrimination tends to benefit the discriminators and that it need not be eroded by market forces.

Yet another explanation of women's jobs and wages is the monopsony (one employer) model (Madden 1975). Employers hiring workers in a competitive labor market have no control over the wage rate.They must take wages as given—determined by the supply of labor and the demand of many other employers also hiring workers in the same labor market. In contrast, a monopsonist (by definition) is the only employer in the labor market. It faces the upward sloping market supply curve and the quantity of labor it demands will affect the market wage rate. Simple graphical analysis of monopsony (see Madden or any of the labor economics texts mentioned above) shows that under these conditions employment and wages will be less than they would be under competitive conditions. Monopsony may be more prevalent in markets for female than male labor because married women are more likely to be geographically restricted to the vicinity of their husband's job than vice versa.

It may also be rational for a monopsonist to segregate the labor force by sex. Paying men and women differing wages for identical work is a blatant violation of the Equal Pay Act and invites law suits by female employees. On the other hand, if women are segregated into different jobs within the firm their lower pay can be rationalized on the ground that the work they do is less valuable (whether it is or not).

In addition, a monopsonist will find it rational to pay women a lower return than men on education and skills. Competition in the market for male labor will ensure that the employer will pay for an additional year of education embodied in male workers as long as its marginal benefit exceeds the market price of education. But if the employer is a monopsonist in the market for female labor, then it will restrict the hiring of educated female workers and depress the returns to education for women.

While examples of pure monopsony are rare, there is some evidence that employer cartels are able to exercise some monopsony power in some labor markets. Ehrenberg and Smith (1982:-46), for example, cite evidence of hospitals colluding to suppress competition among themselves for registered nurses and thus depressing nurses wages below what they would be if each hospital took wages as "given" (that is, as though its quantity demanded had no effect on the market wage). Likewise, there is evidence that large employers of clerical workers in Boston have in the past met regularly to set wage rates for Boston area clerical workers. An investigation by the Massachusetts attorney general resulted in a consent decree in which these employers agreed to stop sharing information on their wage scales for clerical workers.

A final explanation for occupational segregation and low earnings is attributable to Polachek (1979, 1981), who maintains that both result not from discrimination but from choice. Polachek argues that few women expect to remain in the labor force continuously due to the demands of child bearing and rearing. Consequently, they choose jobs that accommodate their family responsibilities—jobs that are close to home or that have flexible hours—or jobs that require relatively little education and training—that are actually "dead end" jobs that neither reward work experience or job tenure nor penalize women for discontinuous work experience. Because women bear and rear children, they *voluntarily* "crowd" into such jobs. The results are occupational concentration, but not forced segregation, and relatively low earnings and earnings growth that result from choice, not discrimination.

The difficulty with this model, as England has pointed out, is that it predicts that women in women's jobs should receive low returns to experience but that women in men's jobs should not (England 1982). In fact, she found no tendency in her data for women in predominantly male jobs to be rewarded more highly for experience (or penalized more severely for discontinuous experience) than were women in predominantly female jobs. Her findings, along with those of Buchele and Aldrich (1985), suggest that *all* women—not just those in women's jobs—earn lower returns to experience than do men. Low wages are apparently not entirely the result of free choices in the labor market.

OCCUPATIONAL SEGREGATION AND COMPARABLE WORTH

All of the above models, as well as others not discussed here, suggest an approach to labor markets that is richer than the simple human capital model. They predict a wage gap between men and women, and under certain assumptions they predict (1) occupational segregation, (2) low earnings in female-dominated jobs, and (3) relatively low returns to human capital for women. At least on the surface therefore they appear entirely consistent with the demand for comparable worth.

Comparable worth is both a diagnosis of the workings of the labor market and a policy prescription to remedy its defects. Advocates assert that women's work is "systematically under-valued" (Steinberg 1984). As the National Academy of Sciences (NAS) study *Women, Work, and Wages* put it,

the work women do is paid less [than men's work], and the more an occupation is dominated by women, the less it pays (Treiman and Hartmann 1981:28)

Analytically, this is entirely consistent with the variant of Becker's model in which employers have a "taste" for discrimination that increases as we move up the occupational hierarchy and that results in lower pay and lower returns to education, training, and experience in women's jobs.

To hypothesize that women's work is devalued could mean at least two things. It might mean that whenever a woman does something, she will be paid less than a man doing the same thing, or it might mean that both men and women doing stereotypically "women's work" will be paid less than either women or men doing what is perceived to be "men's work." The first formulation focuses on pay differences between men and women in the same jobs, and the second focuses on pay differ-ence between workers in female-dominated jobs versus workers in comparable male-dominated (or at least in nonfemale-domi-nated) jobs. Both in the literature and in the instances where comparable worth wage adjustments have actually been imple-mented the second meaning is the one that has been adopted—that women's *jobs* are devalued and women "earn less because they are in *women's jobs*" (Blau 1972:196).

THE CRUCIAL ROLE OF OCCUPATIONAL SEGREGATION

Occupational segregation is therefore at the heart of the com-parable worth diagnosis of women's low wages and the male/female earnings gap. There is certainly little doubt in most ob-servers' minds that the male/female wage gap is largely the result of occupational segregation. England (1981:274), for example, as-serts that

Although women are usually paid less than men in the same occupa-tion, more of the aggregate sex gap in earnings results, because of per-vasive occupational sex segregation, from women's concentration in lower paying occupations.

Another advocate cites the NAS study mentioned above as evidence that

between 35 and 40 percent of the wage gap has been attributed to the segregation of the sexes into different occupations

and concludes that occupational "segregation is the mainstay of the wage gap between the sexes" (Reskin 1984:5).
If occupational segregation is the villain, then comparable worth is the heroine. According to Steinberg and Haignere (1984:13)

comparable worth has evolved to rectify the wage discrimination that is a by-product of occupational segregation

Similarly, Remick (1984:xii) maintains that

The wage differential associated with occupational segregation is the condition that comparable worth attempts to correct.

This emphasis on occupational segregation undoubtedly results from the fact that it is pervasive. As noted in Chapter 1, although occupational segregation is declining, it remains substantial, and studies of the labor force as of 1970 indicate that 65 percent of all workers would have to change jobs to equalize men's and women's occupational distribution (Blau and Hendricks 1979). This focus is also consistent with Becker's model of discrimination, which predicts that women will be employed on jobs where employers have relatively low d values, which is to say that pay discrimination on the job is less important than employment discrimination in obtaining jobs.

As a policy, comparable worth would concentrate on raising wages in women's jobs. While this focus seems plausible and consistent with economic theory, its importance and desirability depend on (1) the premise that occupational segregation is an important cause of women's low wages and (2) the conclusion that raising wages in women's jobs is the best way to deal with the problem of women's low wages.

Raising wages in women's jobs to equal those in "comparable" men's jobs may have adverse consequences depending on which theory of discrimination is correct. If, for example, women are excluded from desirable high-wage jobs and crowded into other jobs as described in Becker or Bergmann's models, simply raising wages in these jobs could reduce employment (Lindsay 1980; Killingsworth 1984). On the other hand, this result need not follow if women's low wages result from employer monopsony power. In this case, forcing employers to pay wages comparable to those on men's jobs will raise female employment.

At any rate, the empirical question of how much comparable worth would raise women's earnings clearly depends on the importance of occupational segregation as a cause of their low earnings. As we have seen, it has come to be an article of faith among advocates of comparable worth that occupational segregation is a major determinant of women's earnings. In the next section we review the evidence on this question.

OCCUPATIONAL SEGREGATION AND WOMEN'S EARNINGS: IS THE QUEEN WEARING ANY CLOTHES?

There is abundant evidence that men and women work in very different jobs and it seems to be widely believed that this is one of main reasons for women's relatively low wages. Of course, dissimilar distributions of men and women across occupations need not imply discrimination. As noted above, Polachek and others have argued that women seek jobs that would be unattractive to most men. But whether one believes that women freely choose the jobs they are in or that they are in those jobs because they have been excluded from the more attractive jobs, almost everyone seems to believe that differences in the occupational distributions of men and women are a major cause of the male/female wage gap.

Although the literature assessing the impact of discrimination on women's wages is vast, the portion that evaluates the importance of occupational segregation is considerably smaller. Several different approaches to the issue have been employed. Some studies have used an accounting method, calculating how much the earnings gap would be reduced if women had the same occupational distribution as men do and if wages within each occupation were unchanged. A shortcoming of this approach is the absence of any controls for human capital and industry differences between male and female workers. Another group of studies uses regression analysis to evaluate the net impact of differences in the occupational distributions of men and women, *controlling* for other effects.

Studies by Blinder (1973), Fuchs (1971), Jusenius (1976), King (1977), Oaxaca (1973), Sanborn (1964), and many others have established beyond any reasonable doubt that the occupational distribution "matters." For example, Jusenius, in a study of women workers, partitioned her sample into three broad occupational skill levels and estimated separate wage equations as a function of human capital, narrow skill category within the skill levels, and a dummy variable indicating whether the occupation was female or not. She found that being in a female job reduced earnings and that being in low-skill jobs reduced the returns to human capital compared to being in a high-skilled job. Other studies, employing different approaches, all confirm this basic conclusion: Differences in occupational distribution account for a statistically significant portion of the wage gap.

In the following pages we review estimates of their *economic* significance—that is, how much difference occupational segregation makes. In general, we find that when occupations are defined at the level that comparable worth advocates usually define them (such as, nurses, plumbers, librarians) only a small part of the gap is due to differences in men's and women's occupational distributions.

The National Academy of Sciences study of *Women, Work, and Wages* employs both of the methods discussed above to estimate the effect of differences in occupational distribution on the male/female earnings gap. Their estimates based on the accounting approach are reproduced in Table 3–1.

Table 3–1 shows the obvious fact that the measured effect of occupational segregation depends crucially on how narrowly "occupation" is defined, with the portion of the gap due to differences in occupational distribution increasing as the classification of occupations becomes more detailed. In the two estimates presented here, for example, the more detailed classification (479 occupations) gives about two times more credit to occupational segregation than does the less detailed one (222 occupations).

These calculations appear to show that occupational segregation accounts for roughly 10 to 20 percent of the earnings gap using a moderately detailed occupational classification and 20 to

Table 3–1. Occupational Segregation in the Earnings Gap

	Number of Occupations	
	222	479
Annual earnings in relation to male earnings		
1. Annual male earnings	100%	100%
2. Women's earnings if they had same earnings as men in each occupation	93	85
3. Men's earnings if they had same earnings as women in each occupation	68	70
4. Annual female earnings	64	63
Percentage of Wage Gap Due to Occupational Segregation		
5. Assuming women get what men are paid [a]	19	41[c]
6. Assuming men get what women are paid [b]	11	19[c]

Source: Treiman and Hartmann (1981: Table 9).

a. Computed as [(1) - (2)]/[(1) - (4)].

b. Computed as [(3) - (4)]/[(1) - (4)].

c. The original table reports values of 39 and 35, rather than 41 and 19, respectively. We have corrected Treiman and Hartmann's calculations on the assumption that the figures in rows 1-4 are acccurate.

40 percent using a more highly detailed classification. But this result is almost surely an overstatement. This is because the NAS study has smuggled an interaction term into its calculation of the effect of occupational segregation. The total male/female earnings gap is caused by (1) differences in pay within occupations, (2) differences in men's and women's occupational distribution, and (3) the interaction of these two causes. This third term is likely to be positive, since occupations in which women are most underrepresented are likely to be those in which the pay gap is the largest. In calculating the effect of occupational segregation as a *residual* (that is, as what is left after pay has been equalized

within occupations), instead of calculating it directly by applying men's occupational distribution to women's wages, the NAS study adds the interaction term to its estimate of the effect of occupational segregation.

A preferable procedure is to assign women the male occupational distribution (or vice versa) and compute the impact on the wage gap directly. These two approaches can result in strikingly different measures of the impact of occupational segregation, as the simple example presented in Table 3–2 indicates. In this example, the unique effect of assigning women men's wages within each occupation is to raise their hourly wages by $2.56 to $6.40. The NAS approach would attribute all of the residual—$2.50 or 49 percent of the wage gap—to occupational segregation. But when we calculate the effect of differences in occupational distributions directly (the alternative method in Table 3–2), we find that it accounts for only $1.50, or 30 percent of the gap. The $1.00 difference represents the interaction of changes in occupational distribution and intraoccupational wages, and this effect cannot be uniquely assigned to either of the other two.[2]

Mary Stevenson (1975) undertook a methodologically similar study. She developed seventeen different occupation levels (occlevel) based on *Dictionary of Occupational Titles (DOT)* job requirements and computed the distribution of men and women across these levels. She then estimated the impact of assigning women the same occupational distribution as men and described her findings as follows:

changing their [white women's] distribution across occlevels to match that of white males would do virtually nothing to boost their relative wages. Giving white women the white male average wage in each occlevel would bring white women very close to parity with white men (Stevenson 1975:189).

Stevenson's results may be due to her use of too few and too aggregative job categories, or perhaps unequal pay within job categories really is more important than the job distribution. There is no way of knowing based on her analysis. Nevertheless, she concludes that

almost all the difference in wages . . . may be attributed to occupational segregation *within* occlevels (Stevenson 1975:189).

Table 3–2. The Effect of the Interaction Term on Alternative Estimates of the Impact of Occupational Segregation (a hypothetical example).

Occupation	Men		Women	
	Percentage	Wage	Percentage	Wage
1	60%	$10.00	10%	$6.00
2	30	8.00	30	4.80
3	10	5.00	60	3.00
	$\overline{W}^m = \$8.90$		$\overline{W}^f = \$3.84$	

$$\text{GAP} = \$5.06$$

NAS method:
  $\overline{W}^f$ if women had men's wages in each occupation: $6.40
  Remaining gap due to occupational segregation: $8.90 − 6.40 = $2.50
  Percentage of gap due to occupational segregation: 2.50/5.06 = 49%
Alternative method:
  $\overline{W}^f$ if women had men's occupational distribution: $5.34
  Increase in $\overline{W}^f$ due to elimination of occupational segregation: $5.34 − 3.84 = $1.50
  Percentage of gap due to occupational segregation: 1.50/5.06 = 30%

Although her results indicate that, based on her analytical categories, occupational segregation has no effect on women's wages, Stevenson's article is commonly cited in subsequent works as evidence of the importance of occupational segregation in the male/female earnings gap.

As mentioned above, the value of the econometric studies is that they allow the researcher to control for (at least some) differences between men and women that are correlated with occupation and earnings and thus to better isolate the *net effect* of occupational segregation on the wage gap. For example, just as part of the earnings gap is due to women, on the average, having fewer years of work experience than men, part of the difference in their occupational distributions is most likely due to differences in their experience. Thus, even if equal employment opportunity existed and even if men and women did not vary systematically in their occupational preferences, "human capital" differences would produce *some* (albeit, possibly small) difference in their occupational distributions.

Two econometric studies that developed occupational attainment models to measure the effect of occupational segregation on the male/female earnings gap are those of Brown, Moon, and Zolith (1980) and Buchele (1981). Each of these studies first estimated an occupational attainment model to obtain the probability of employment in each occupational category as a function of individuals' human capital levels and other attributes. They then estimated separate wage equations by sex for each occupation and estimated the impact on the wage gap of assigning women according to the male occupational attainment model. While these studies are analytically more sophisticated than the others reviewed here, they employ too few occupational categories to provide a definitive assessment of the importance of occupational segregation. Nevertheless, their results are of interest because their occupational categories correspond roughly to the separate categories used in job evaluation (which would be merged in a comparable worth study). Brown *et al.* (1980:18), for example, concluded that

[e]liminating differences by sex across broad occupational categories will have little impact on women's wage rates unless it is accompanied by changes in relative wage rates within occupations

and Buchele (1981:223) found that

while job segregation is pervasive, it does not directly explain why women earn less than men do.

A second econometric approach, undertaken by Roos (1981), estimated individual men's and women's earnings equations, which included a number of occupational characteristics (variables measuring autonomy and control over other workers, occupational status, and median male earnings) as well as percentage of workers in the occupation who are women. Roos found differential returns to occupational traits and to percent female[3] for men and women and estimated that the earnings gap would decrease by about 13 percent if women were assigned men's values for these variables.

Roos's calculation of the effect on women's earnings of giving them men's occupational characteristics suffers from a logical flaw (shared with some of the other studies discussed above), however. Since men tend to be employed in occupations in which the average percent female is less than it is for the labor force as a whole, it is not logically possible for *all* women to work in occupations that have the same percent females as the average male worker presently does.

A variation on this approach estimates the impact on *occupational wages* of the percent female in the occupation. In the NAS study by Treiman and Hartmann and in later work by Treiman, Hartmann, and Roos the occupational wage (that is, the weighted average wage of both men and women in each occupation) was regressed on percent female in the occupation, both alone and controlling for worker and job characteristics. The NAS study concluded that "the more an occupation is dominated by women, the less it pays" (Treiman and Hartmann 1981:28). Similarly, the study by Treiman, Hartmann, and Roos (1981:144) announced that

The coefficient associated with percent female can be interpreted as a direct measure of discrimination.

Actually, these estimates provide no evidence at all about occupational segregation, since a negative coefficient on percent female will be found even in the complete absence of occupational segregation (unless men and women within each occupation are paid the same). Suppose, for example, that all women were paid exactly $6 per hour and all men were paid exactly $10 per hour, regardless of their occupation. Whatever the distribution of men and women across occupations, the male/female earnings ratio will be .6; the occupational distribution of men and women has no effect on the male/female wage gap. But the sex composition of employment in an occupation will profoundly affect the mean wage of workers in that occupation. Occupations that are 90 percent male and 10 percent female will have an average wage of $9.60 per hour, while occupations that are 90 percent female and 10 percent male will have a mean wage of only $6.40 per hour. Thus, percent female will have a large, statistically significant effect on occupational wages, even though the average wages of men and women in any occupation are (in this hypothetical example) entirely independent of sex composition of the occupation. In short, the authors have mistaken a statistical artifact (the weighted average) for a behaviorial relationship.

Moreover, as was briefly noted in the last chapter, when the Treiman, Hartmann, Roos model was estimated separately for male- and female-dominated occupations, the coefficients for all but one of the explanatory variables were *higher* in women's than in men's jobs. Undaunted, the authors simply ignored this result, which seems to suggest that women's jobs pay *higher* returns to worker skills and job skill requirements than do men's jobs. This is a conclusion that can hardly be congenial to those who stress occupational segregation as a cause of women's low earnings.

A study that is methodologically similar to these last two, but that avoids the statistical pitfall discussed above, was undertaken by England, Chassie, and McCormack (1982). They regressed median occupational earnings of full-time, year-round male and female workers on a set of *Dictionary of Occupational Titles' (DOT)* job characteristics plus the percentage of the occupation that was female. On the basis of their regression results we estimate that if men and women were represented in each occupation in proportion to their percentage in the total sample, the wage gap would be reduced by 28 percent.

This is almost certainly an overestimate because the equations used to estimate the effect of percent female on men's and women's occupational wages contained no controls for workers' human capital or for industry of employment. And as we shall see below, inclusion of these variables have a substantial impact on the estimated effect of percent female on occupational wages.

NEW FINDINGS ON THE IMPORTANCE OF OCCUPATIONAL SEGREGATION

As the above discussion should have made clear, the literature on the role of occupational segregation in the male/female earnings gap is unsatisfactory on many counts. Yet it is widely cited as evidence that occupational segregation is an important, perhaps the most important, cause of the wage gap and as justification for a comparable worth approach to reducing the wage gap. For this reason we undertake here our own analysis of the importance of occupational segregation, based on a model that we believe avoids the problems discussed above.

Our data come from the National Longitudinal Surveys (NLS) of men and women undertaken during 1980 and on the *Dictionary of Occupational Titles* (DOT) survey of job requirements. Our sample of individuals from the NLS contains 1,856 male and 1,-441 female nonagricultural employees who worked at least twenty hours per week for at least thirteen weeks in 1980. Respondents classified as managers, officials, and proprietors not elsewhere classified were dropped from the sample because this occupational category is notoriously heterogeneous in terms of the range of positions and pay they entail, and the ensuing analysis depends on our having reasonably clearly defined occupational categories. Likewise sales persons were split into two groups depending on whether they worked in manufacturing or wholesale trade, on one hand, or retail trade, on the other. The men in the sample ranged from age 28 to 38 at the time of the survey, while the women were from age 26 to 36.

The *DOT* data provide information on a wide range of job skill requirements, working conditions, and other demands of the job. Because many of these characteristics are highly duplicative, we performed a factor analysis on the original data that collapsed them into three factors that account for over 60 percent of the variance of the underlying *DOT* measures. These factors were then used to compute factor scores for each occupation, which provided three statistically independent measures of requirements of each NLS respondent's job. We have used these factor scores in some subsidiary analysis that we will report on in the next chapter. But in our main analysis we have retained only two of the *DOT* measures—the general education development (GED) and specific vocational preparation (SVP) requirements of the job. We have done this to avoid the problems created by using arbitrarily scaled variables (such as factor scores) discussed in Chapter 2. Our variables are defined and described in Tables 3–3 and 3–4.

To gauge the impact of occupational segregation we estimate separately the determinants of men's and women's occupational wages. The dependent variable is the mean wage of all males (females) in the occupation. Thus, for example, we have one ob-

Table 3–3. Definitions of Variables.

Symbol	Definition
WAGE	Hourly wage rate
PFEM	Percent female in occupation
PBLK	Percent black in occupation
SCH	Years of schooling completed
XPR	Work experience since leaving school prior to current job (in years)
TEN	Tenure with current employer (in years)
GED	The general educational development of respondent's occupation measured in equivalent years of schooling [a]
SVP	The specific vocational preparation requirement measured in equivalent years of work experience [a]
GOVT	Equals 1 if employed in government; 0 otherwise
CBRG	Equals 1 if wage set by collective bargaining; 0 otherwise
CORE	Equals 1 if employed in a "core" industry; 0 otherwise [b]
PERF	Equals 1 if employed in "peripheral" industry; 0 otherwise [b]
SO	Equals 1 if resides in South; 0 otherwise
SMSA	Equals 1 if resides in Standard Metropolitan Statistical Area; 0 otherwise

a. See Scovill (1966).

b. Based on a factor analysis of manufacturing, mining construction and transportation, communication, and public utility industries. Core industries are those characterized by high product market concentration, large establishment size, and high capital labor ratios and profit rates. Peripheral industries are their antithesis. See Buchele (1983).

servation on the mean wage of all forty-three female secondary school teachers in the sample and another on the mean wage of all fifty-one male secondary school teachers in the sample. Our 3,297 observations on individual wages are thus reduced to 316 observations on the mean occupational wages of men and women. All of the independent variables in the model are defined analogously (for example, the mean years of schooling of

Table 3–4. Means of Variables.

Variable	Total	Men	Women
WAGE	7.04	8.36	5.33
PFEM	.437	.224	.712
PBLK	.255	.247	.267
SCH	13.14	13.26	12.99
XPR	5.02	5.55	4.34
TEN	5.81	6.40	5.05
GED	11.68	11.68	11.69
SVP	1.86	2.21	1.42
GOVT	.224	.197	.260
CBRG	.360	.399	.310
CORE	.174	.211	.128
PERF	.255	.335	.153
SO	.429	.420	.439
SMSA	.697	.700	.693
N (individuals)	3,297	1,856	1,441

all female secondary school teachers comprises a single observation on years of schooling for that particular group), with the exception of percent female for the occupation—the variable used to measure an occupation's "gender" (see Johnson and Solon 1984 for a similar approach).

We report estimates based on a number of regression equations ranging from a simple regression of occupational wages on percent female through more complete specifications that include controls for worker and job traits, industry and region of employment, and finally, interactions of percent female with all other independent variables. The four basic equations, estimated separately for men and women, are then

$$\overline{W}_i^s = a^s + b^s F_i \tag{3.1}$$

$$\overline{W}_i^s = a^s + b^s F_i + \Sigma_j c_j^s \overline{T}_{ij}^s \tag{3.2}$$

$$\overline{W}_i^s = a^s + b^s F_i + \Sigma_j c_j^s \overline{T}_{ij}^s + \Sigma_j d_j^s \overline{C}_{ij}^s \tag{3.3}$$

$$\overline{W}_i^s = a^s + b^s F_i + \Sigma_j c_j^s \overline{T}_{ij}^s + \Sigma_j d_j^s \overline{C}_{ij}^s + \Sigma_j g_j^s F_i \overline{T}_{ij}^s + \Sigma_j h_j^s F_i \overline{C}_{ij}^s \tag{3.4}$$

where $\overline{W}_i^s$ is the mean wage for sex s in occupation i,
F_i is the percent female in the occupation i,

$\overline{T}^s_{ij}$ is the mean level of job/worker trait j for sex s in occupation i, and

$\overline{C}^s_{ij}$ is the mean level of industry/regional control j for sex s in occupation i.

Estimates of these equations are presented in Tables 3–5a and 3–5b.[4] We focus here on the estimates of the coefficient of percent female in the occupation (PFEM). Column 1 in each table indicates that a 100 percent difference in percent female is associated with a $.95 difference in the average occupational wages of men and a $1.16 difference in the average occupational wages of women. The addition of the job/worker traits in column 2 substantially reduces the coefficient of PFEM for men but not for women. In contrast, the addition of industry and regional controls in column 3 sharply reduces the impact of percent female for women but not for men.

Finally, column 4 gives the coefficients of all the interaction terms in the full model. These are presented because they are used to calculate our estimates of the effect of male/female differences in the occupational distribution on the male/female wage gap. We note here only that the coefficients are quite different for men and women. This suggests that perhaps the effect of an occupation's femaleness on its wage rate depends on the *kind* of occupation we are talking about (as described by the right-hand variables) and also that this works quite differently for men and women.

Table 3–6 contains alternative estimates of the impact on the wage gap of assigning men and women to occupations in proportion to their representation in the sample—that is, making all occupations 43.7 percent female. (Note that our sample is quite close to the 1980 labor force national average of 43.2 percent female.) We see that eliminating differences in occupational distributions (but holding constant occupational wages) reduces the $3.03 wage gap by $.52 (or 17.2 percent), if we do not control for other causes of differences in occupational wages. This effect declines to only $.31 (or 10.1 percent) when we add controls for job/worker traits and industry and region but rises back up to $.46 (or 15.3 percent) when we allow percent female to interact with the other variables. We conclude that male/female differ-

Table 3–5a. The Effect on Men's Wages of Percent Female in the Occupation (Dependent Variable: Mean Male Wages in the Occupation).

Equation Number	(1)	(2)	(3)	(4)
PFEM	− 0.952	− 0.691	− 0.686	1.085
PFEM*PBLK				.642
PFEM*SCH				.164
PFEM*XPR				.058
PFEM*TEN				.187
PFEM*GED				− .393
PFEM*SVP				.193
PFEM*GOVT				.140
PFEM*CBRG				− .687[a]
PFEM*CORE				− 1.277
PFEM*PERF				− 3.970
PFEM*SO				− 1.574
PFEM*SMSA				1.151
N (occupations) = 192				

a. Denotes significance at the .05 level in a one-tailed test.

Note 1. Equation (1) is a simple regression of occupational wages on percent female in the occupation. Equation (2) adds the control variables PBLK, SCH, XPR, TEN, GED, SVP. Equation (3) adds the additional controls GOVT, CORE, PERF, CBRG, SO, and SMSA. Equation (4) includes all of these plus their interaction with percent female as listed in the left-hand column.

Note 2. The unit of observation is the detailed occupation. Thus, the 1,856 men in our sample are employed in 192 different occupations, giving a sample size of 192 for these regressions. The variables in these regressions are occupational means—that is, they are the mean values for all the men in the occupation. The equations are estimated by weighted least squares, as described in footnote 4.

ences in occupational distribution account for something like 15 percent of the male/female wage gap. This is a significant figure but far less than the comparable worth advocates cited above seem to believe.

CONCLUSION

It is clear that comparable worth, as a diagnosis of women's earnings, is entirely consistent with several economic theories of

Table 3–5b. The Effect on Women's Wage of Percent Female in the Occupation (Dependent Variable: Mean Female Wages in the Occupation).

Equation Number	(1)	(2)	(3)	(4)
PFEM	− 1.156[b]	− 1.063[b]	− 0.586	− 13.861[a]
PFEM*PBLK				3.372
PFEM*SCH				.604
PFEM*XPR				.294
PFEM*TEN				.222
PFEM*GED				.293
PFEM*SVP				.322
PFEM*GOVT				− 3.709[a]
PFEM*CBRG				1.121
PFEM*CORE				1.129
PFEM*PERF				− 1.154
PFEM*SO				1.713
PFEM*SMSA				− 1.085
N (occupations) = 124				

a. Denotes significance at the .05 level in a one-tailed test.
b. Denotes significance at the .01 level in a one-tailed test.
Note 1. See Table 3–5a.
Note 2. The unit of observation is the detailed occupation. Thus, the 1,441 women in the sample are employed in 124 different occupations, giving a sample size of 124 for these regressions. The variables in these regressions are occupational means—that is, they are the mean values for all women in the occupation. The equations are estimated by weighted least squares as described in end of chapter note 4.

discrimination. Where discrimination exists, rather than simple profit-maximizing behavior, intervention in the wage determination process can potentially improve the fairness of current labor market outcomes without reducing economic efficiency.

If we interpret comparable worth as a correction for the devaluation of women's work and we use percent female in an occupation as a measure of the extent to which it is perceived to be a woman's job, then the question of the impact of comparable worth is closely tied to the issue of the importance of occupation-

Table 3–6. Effect on the Male/Female Wage Gap of Distributing Men and Women Equally across All Occupations.

	1	*2*	*3*	*4*
Dollars	− $.521	− $.439	− $.307	− $.462
Percentage	− 17.2%	− 14.5%	− 10.1%	− 15.3%

Note: Computed from data in Tables 3–5a and 3–5b by calculating the effect of moving men from occupations that average 22.4 percent female (the mean percentage of females for all men) to ones that are 43.7 percent female (the mean percentage of females for the whole sample) and moving women from occupations that are 71.2 percent female (the mean for all women) to ones that are also 43.7 percent female. Men's average earnings are $8.36, women's are $5.33; the gap is $3.03.

al segregation in the male/female gap. Although widely cited, the existing research assessing the effect of occupational segregation on the wage gap is too flawed to support a definitive conclusion on this question. Our own findings suggest that occupational segregation has a small but not insignificant effect on the male/female wage gap. And this, in turn, implies that comparable worth may have neither as large a beneficial impact on the wage gap as its supporters have claimed nor as large a detrimental effect on employment as its detractors have charged.

NOTES

1. This is strictly true only under constant returns to training, or a linear wage/training function. If the relationship were highly nonlinear (that is, if there were strongly increasing or decreasing returns to training) and if different groups of workers differed widely in the amount of training they had, nondiscriminatory differences in returns to training between different groups of workers could exist.
2. We acknowledge that our approach, which excludes the interaction effect from the calculation of the effect of occupational segregation on the wage gap, errs in the opposite direction of the NAS approach. In fact, there is no way to know what share of the interaction term "belongs" to each of the two other terms. But this does not justify ignoring it or arbitrarily including it in one of the terms.
3. In the remainder of this book the phrase "percentage of workers in the occupation who are women" will be abbreviated "percent female in the occupation" or simply "percent female."
4. Since the observed occupation/sex means are calculated from different sample sizes (depending on the number of men and women in our sample in each occu-

pation), the error variance will not be constant across observations. Occupational means based on relatively few individuals observations will have relatively large error variances, and ordinary least squares regression (which minimizes the sum of squared "errors") will place disproportionate weight on these least precisely measured observations. Unequal error variances, or heteroscedasticity, causes ordinary least squares estimates of the standard errors of estimated parameters to be biased and this invalidates the standard tests of significance.

Weighted least squares regression is used to correct for heteroscedasticity in these equations. Each observation is weighted by the square root of the number of individuals in the occupation, and the constant term is replaced by the weight, according to standard procedures for grouped data (Maddala 1977:268–74). R-squares are not reported, since they are spuriously inflated by this weighting procedure.

BIBLIOGRAPHY

Becker, Gary. 1964. *Human Capital.* New York: National Bureau of Economic Research.
_____ . 1957. *The Economics of Discrimination.* Chicago: University of Chicago.
Bergmann, Barbara. 1971. "The Effect on White Incomes of Discrimination in Employment." *Journal of Political Economy* 79 (March/April):294–313.
Blau, Francine D. 1972. " 'Women's Place' in the Labor Market." *American Economics Review* 62 (May):192–97.
Blau, Francine, and Wallace Hendricks. 1979. "Occupational Segregation by Sex: Trends and Prospects." *Journal of Human Resources* 14 (Spring):197–210
Blau, Francine, and Carol Jusenius. 1976. "Economist's Approaches to Sex Segregation in the Labor Market: An Appraisal." In *Women in the Work Place,* edited by Martha Blaxall and Barbara Reagan, pp. 181–99. Chicago: University of Chicago Press.
Blaug, Mark. 1976. "Human Capital Theory: A Slightly Jaundiced Survey." *Journal of Economic Literature* 14 (Sept.):827–55.
Blinder, Alan S. 1973. "Wage Discrimination: Reduced Form and Structural Estimates." *Journal of Human Resources* 8 (Fall):436–55.
Brown, Randall; Marilyn Moon; and Barbara Zoloth. 1980. "Incorporating Occupational Attainment in Studies of Male/Female Earnings Differentials." *Journal of Human Resources* 15 (Winter):3–28.
Buchele, Robert. 1981. "Sex Discrimination and Labor Market Segmentation." In *The Dynamics of Labor Market Segmentation,* edited by Frank Wilkinson, pp. 211–27. London: Academic Press.
_____ . 1983. "Economic Dualism and Employment Discrimination." *Industrial Relations* (Fall):410–18.
Buchele, Robert, and Mark Aldrich. 1985. "How Much Difference Would Comparable Worth Make?" *Industrial Relations* 24 (Spring):222–33.
Daily Hampshire Gazette. 1985. Northampton, Mass.
Daily Labor Report. 1984. Washington, D.C.: Bureau of National Affairs, Inc.

Ehrenberg, Ronald, and Robert Smith. 1982. *Modern Labor Economics.* Glenview, Ill.: Scott, Foresman.

England, Paula. 1981. "Assessing Trends in Occupational Sex Segregation, 1900 –1976." In *Sociological Perspectives on Labor Markets,* edited by Ivar Berg, pp. 273–95. New York: Academic Press.

———. 1982. "The Failure of Human Capital Theory to Explain Occupational Sex Discrimination." *Journal of Human Resources* 17 (Summer):358–69.

———. 1984. "Socioeconomic Explanations of Job Segregation." In *Comparable Worth and Wage Discrimination,* edited by Helen Remick, pp. 28–46. Philadelphia: Temple University Press.

England, Paula; Marilyn Chassie; and Linda McCormack. 1982. "Skill Demands and Earnings in Female and Male Occupations." *Sociology and Social Research* 66 (Jan.):147–68.

Fuchs, Victor. 1971. "Differences in Hourly Earnings between Men and Women." *Monthly Labor Review* 94 (May):9–15.

Hammermesh, Daniel, and Albert Rees. 1984. *The Economics of Work and Pay.* New York: Harper & Row.

Johnson, George, and Gary Solon. 1984. "Pay Differences between Women's Jobs and Men's Jobs: The Empirical Foundations of Comparable Worth Legislation." *National Bureau of Economic Research* Working Paper No. 1472 (Sept.).

Jusenius, Carol. 1976. "The Influence of Work Experience, Skill Requirement, and Occupational Segregation on Women's Earnings." *Journal of Economics and Business* 29:107–15.

Killingsworth, Mark R. 1984. "Statement on Comparable Worth." Testimony before the Joint Economic Committee, U.S. Congress. 98th Cong., 2d. Sess. (April 10).

King, Allan. 1977. "Is Occupational Segregation the Cause of the Flatter Experience Earnings Profiles of Women?" *Journal of Human Resources* 12 (Fall):541–59.

Lindsay, Cotton Mather. 1980. "Equal Pay for Comparable Work." University of Miami Law and Economics Center Occasional Paper.

Maddala, G.S. 1977. *Econometrics.* New York: McGraw Hill.

Madden, Janice. 1975. "Discrimination—A Manifestation of Male Market Power?" In *Sex Discrimination and the Division of Labor,* edited by Cynthia Lloyd, pp. 146–74. New York: Columbia University Press.

Mincer, Jacob. 1962. "On-the-Job Training: Costs, Returns, and Implications." *Journal of Political Economy Supplement* 70 (Oct.):50–79.

———. 1974. *Schooling, Experience, and Earnings.* New York: NBER.

New York Times. 1982–1985.

Oaxaca, Ronald. 1973. "Male–Female Wage Differentials in Urban Labor Markets." *International Economic Review* (Oct.):693–709.

Polachek, Solomon. 1979. "Occupational Segregation among Women: Theory, Evidence, and a Prognosis." In *Women in the Labor Market,* edited by Cynthia Lloyd, pp. 137–57. New York: Columbia University Press.

———. 1981. "Occupational Self-Selection: A Human Capital Approach to Sex Differences in Occupational Structure." *Review of Economics and Statistics* (Feb.):60–69.

Reich, Michael. 1981. *Racial Inequality*. Princeton: Princeton University Press.

Remick, Helen. 1984. "Preface." In *Comparable Worth and Wage Discrimination*, edited by Helen Remick, p. xii. Philadelphia: Temple University Press.

Reskin, Barbara. 1984. "Sex Segregation in the Workplace." In *Gender at Work*, pp. 1–12. Washington, D.C.: Women's Research and Education Institute.

Roos, Patricia. 1981. "Sex Stratification in the Workplace: Male–Female Differences in Economic Returns to Occupation." *Social Science Research* 10:-195–223.

Sanborn, Henry. 1964. "Pay Differentials between Men and Women." *Industrial and Labor Relations Review* 17 (July):534–50.

Scovill, James. 1966. "Education and Training Requirements for Occupations." *Review of Economics and Statistics* (Nov.):387–94.

Shepela, Sharon T., and Ann T. Viviano. 1984. "Some Psychological Factors Affecting Job Segregation and Wages." In *Comparable Worth and Wage Discrimination*, edited by Helen Remick, pp. 47–58. Philadelphia: Temple University Press.

Steinberg, Ronnie. 1984. " 'A Want of Harmony': Perspectives on Wage Discrimination and Comparable Worth." In *Comparable Worth and Wage Discrimination*, edited by Helen Remick, pp. 3–27. Philadelphia: Temple University Press.

Steinberg, Ronnie, and Lois Haignere. 1984. "Separate but Equivalent: Equal Pay for Work of Comparable Worth." In *Gender at Work*, pp. 13–26. Washington, D. C.: Women's Research and Education Institute.

Stevenson, Mary. 1975. "Relative Wages and Sex Segregation by Occupation." In *Sex Discrimination and the Division of Labor*, edited by Cynthia Lloyd, pp. 175–200. New York: Columbia University Press.

Treiman, Donald, and Heidi Hartmann. 1981. *Women, Work, and Wages*. Washington, D.C.: National Academy Press.

Treiman, D.; H. Hartmann; and P. Roos. 1984. "Assessing Pay Discrimination Using National Data." In *Comparable Worth and Wage Discrimination*, edited by Helen Remick, pp. 137–54. Philadelphia: Temple University Press.

CHAPTER 4

The Economic Implications of Comparable Worth

If you can define fairness you ought to be canonized.
-LINDA CHAVEZ, staff director of U.S. Commission on Civil Rights.
(*Washington Post*, April 5, 1985:A2)

[Job rating] is done every day by American business and industry.
-ELEANOR HOLMES NORTON, former chairwoman of the Equal Employment Opportunity Commission (*New York Times*, Sept. 4, 1984:B9)

INTRODUCTION

This chapter develops a model of comparable worth in terms of the economic theory of compensating wage differentials. The claim that workers in "women's jobs" do not receive equal pay for comparable work is interpreted to mean they are not paid the same compensating wage differentials as are other workers. We specify two alternative models of comparable worth: (1) an "advocate's model," which is shown to be susceptible to critics' claims that comparable worth "violates the laws of supply and demand," and (2) an "economist's model," which is not. Both models are used to estimate the impact of comparable worth on earnings in "women's jobs" and on the male/female wage gap.

A THEORY OF COMPARABLE WORTH

Although the case for comparable worth is usually stated in normative terms, it is not inconsistent with economic efficiency if one is willing to accept the proposition that individuals ought not to be allowed to indulge a taste for discrimination. As we argued at the beginning of the last chapter, a labor market that is both nondiscriminating and competitive would pay wages that reflect workers' productivity, not their gender. All jobs would pay the same returns to training and to all other compensable traits (such as education, experience, special skill requirements). In Figure 3–1, Job *B* pays more than Job *A* because it requires more training, but it pays the same wage increment for an additional unit of training, that is, it pays the same *returns* to training.[1] In the absence of barriers to mobility workers will move among jobs, and employers will bid for workers until all differences in returns to jobs traits are eliminated.

For example, suppose that job *i* is characterized by a set of job traits such that the more demanding or unattractive the job is on trait *j*, the greater the value of T_{ij}. (Desirable job traits that act as nonpecuniary income can be handled in this scheme by defining them in terms of their opposites.) The locus of tangencies, $W(T_j)$, shown in Figure 4–1, represents the market clearing, equilibrium wage differential among jobs that differ only with respect to trait *j*. At these points of tangency between workers' indifference curves and employers' iso-profit curves the slope of $W(T_j)$ equals both the worker's and the employer's marginal rate of substitution between pay and job trait *j*. That is, it represents both the value to workers of a marginal reduction in trait *j* and the marginal cost to employers of making that reduction.[2]

Thus, supply and demand in such a labor market will establish *compensating wage differentials* between two jobs that reflect the responses of workers on the margin to their associated job traits (Smith 1979; Thaler and Rosen 1975). Because these differentials result from voluntary actions, we can assume that they make both workers and employers better off. This is the basis of the economists' conclusion that competitive markets, by equalizing marginal returns, will bring about an efficient, welfare maximizing matching of jobs and workers.

If any group of workers (such as women) is denied access to the full range of jobs and crowded into a subset of jobs, the wages of all workers in those occupations are likely to be depressed. Likewise, the compensating wage differential or wage increment received by workers in those jobs for a unit of trait *j* is likely to be reduced below the differential associated with trait *j* in other jobs. The locus of compensating wage differentials on job trait *j* for individuals in female jobs, $Wf(T_j)$, will lie below the

Figure 4–1. The Compensating Wage Differential or Marginal Return to Job Trait j.

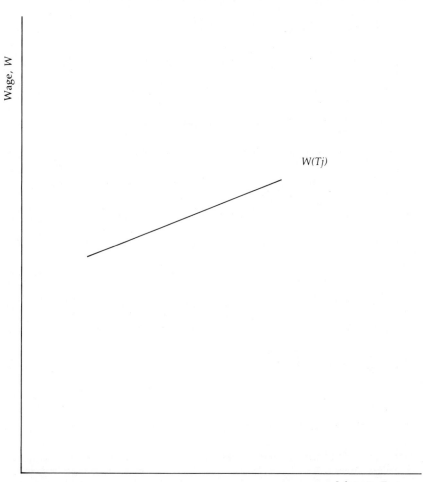

Wage, W

$W(Tj)$

Job trait, T_j

corresponding locus for male jobs, $W^m(T_j)$, as depicted in Figure 4–2. In effect, the sex composition of an occupation becomes a job trait that yields a compensating wage differential. We cannot say that this result is inefficient in the sense that a different arrangement could make everyone better off. After all, ending discrimination would surely make the discriminators worse off in their own terms. But a comparable worth adjustment that eliminates wage differentials based on the sex composition of occupa-

Figure 4–2. Sex Discrimination and Compensating Wage Differentials.

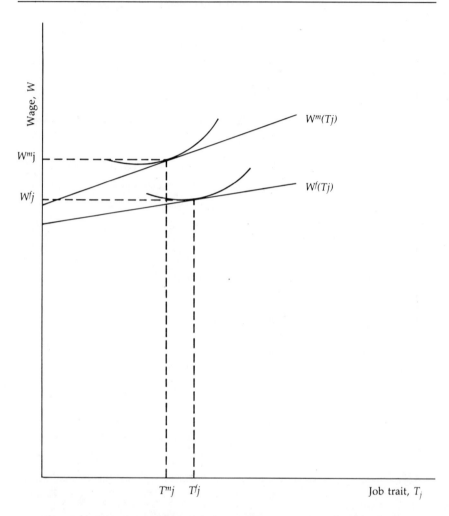

tions is a necessary condition for a labor market that is *both* non-discriminatory and efficient.

The above analysis helps clarify a number of issues that have surrounded the comparable worth debate. Comparable worth is sometimes defined to mean equal pay for different but comparable *jobs*—rather than equal *returns to job traits*, as we have defined it here. Critics have responded by arguing that trying to compare jobs is like comparing apples and oranges (Killingsworth 1985b). Others have claimed that comparable worth ostensibly violates the laws of supply and demand (Bunzel 1982). In the light of the above model we address these and other criticisms of comparable worth in the next section of this chapter.

DOES COMPARABLE WORTH MAKE ECONOMIC SENSE?

Many of the arguments against comparable worth concern two specific technical and economic criticisms. Claims that comparable worth is both subjective and arbitrary—like comparing apples and oranges—reflect technical arguments about job evaluation. And as we saw in Chapter 2, these criticisms have some merit when applied to comparable worth job evaluations as presently practiced. Assertions that comparable worth would violate the laws of supply and demand reflect concerns that labor shortages and surpluses will be created in different occupations if any agency other than "market forces" sets wages. We evaluate these criticisms and assess their effect on the two models of comparable worth that we present in the next section of this chapter.

APPLES AND ORANGES?

Opponents of comparable worth have argued that trying to compare the worth of different jobs on the basis of a common set of job traits is like trying to compare the value of apples and oranges on the basis of their nutritional content. They argue that subjective consumer tastes obviously play a large part in determining the demand for, and therefore the price of, apples and oranges. As a result, even if the two fruits were identical in their nutritional content this does not imply that they would fetch the same price in a perfectly competitive market (Killingsworth 1985b:94).

It is true that the market does not mandate equal prices for foods with comparable nutritional and caloric content; nor does it require equal pay for jobs with comparable level of skill, effort, and responsibility. But as we showed above, it does require equal marginal *returns* to given levels of these traits. Thus, for example, to the extent that the price of both apples and oranges is affected at all by the fact that they are both sources of (say) vitamin C, we would expect them to earn equal marginal returns to given levels of that trait. And we would expect the *net* effect of higher levels of vitamin C in oranges to raise the price of oranges relative to apples. However, this does *not* mean that even if oranges dominated apples on every objectively measurable trait, they would or should sell for a higher price. This is so because there are unmeasured qualitative differences between apples and oranges—perhaps their distinctive "essences;" that affect consumer demand for them. Realistically, it is not possible for any fruit (or job) evaluation system to take account of all the relevant differences between apples and oranges (or between substantively different jobs).

Separate regression equations for apples and oranges that estimate their prices as a function of their common properties would undoubtedly attribute a large part of the "price gap" between them to differences in the constant terms of their respective equations. This represents the difference in the average price of apples and oranges that is *unexplained* by their measured qualities. Similarly, wage equations also typically attribute some of the difference between men's and women's earnings to differences in levels of, and returns to, job traits and some of it to differences in constant terms. Since equal returns to job traits are a necessary condition of efficient, nondiscriminating labor markets, it would make sense to adjust wage differences for any such differential returns. But there is no basis in economic theory for equating the constant terms in these equations. To continue the analogy, we would expect a competitive market to generate equal returns to vitamin C, whether embodied in an apple or an orange. But we would not expect separate regression equations that expressed the prices of apples and oranges as a function of their nutritional qualities to have the same constant terms. Similarly, even in a nondiscriminatory labor market, we cannot expect the wage equations for men's and women's jobs to have identical constant terms. And to assign the wage equation for women's jobs the constant term from the equation for men's jobs is, as critics charge, like describing an apple as an orange with a somewhat different set of vitamins and minerals.

SUPPLY AND DEMAND?

Leaving apples and oranges aside, we turn to the charge often levied by critics, that comparable worth violates the laws of supply and demand. As noted, we agree with critics' claims that comparable worth is "fatally flawed" when it is expressed as equal pay for comparable *jobs*. But if comparable worth is defined to imply *equal returns to job traits*, this objection loses much of its force. As we argued above, a competitive, nondiscriminating market would, in equilibrium, result in all workers receiving equal marginal returns to given levels of job traits. Thus, unless it can be shown that returns to job traits are highly nonlinear and men's and women's jobs have very different levels of these traits (which we argue below is unlikely), then a wage adjustment that equalizes returns would improve—not undermine—the workings of the market (wages would then better approximate the wage structure generated by a competitive, nondiscriminatory market).

Yet this argument does not entirely meet critics' objections because it deals with equilibrium marginal returns to job or personal traits, and the market may well not be—and probably never is—in long-run equilibrium. Surely it is difficult to argue that the relatively low returns to (say) education that have characterized women's jobs for decades result from supply/demand disequilibria. But might not a comparable worth rule prevent the market from responding to short-run disequilibrium? Suppose for example that a defense buildup were to increase the demand for machinists—a largely male trade. Employers would respond by bidding up the returns to this type of training. But a rigid comparable worth rule, unless it were sensitive to qualitative differences in skills, rather than just quantitative differences in training time, might require an increase in returns to nursing training too—and this is clearly the "wrong" signal.

We conclude that on this level the critics' point is well taken and that wage adjustments that are intended to correct for persistently low returns to job traits in women's jobs need to be applied flexibly. Employers need to be able to offer relatively high (or low) returns for some kinds of skills and training in response to short-run fluctuations in demand or supply. At least one advocate (Remick 1985) has acknowledged this. But she has cautioned that both the principle of comparable worth and the laws of supply and demand require that these exceptions be *temporary*. An efficient market should automatically eliminate supply-demand disequilibria and resulting differential returns to job traits. Such flexibility might be easier to achieve in a collective bargaining arrangement than as a matter of law. This is another reason why—as we have noted above—comparable worth is much more threatening to employers as public policy (law) than it is as a negotiable union demand.

PRACTICE

Another criticism of comparable worth is aimed at the entire concept of job evaluation. Thus it is claimed that job evaluation substitutes the inherently subjective judgment of a job evaluator for actual worker preferences. Killingsworth (1985a), for example, evokes Albert Rees's critique of Adam Smith's argument that butchering must pay a wage premium in order to attract workers to that trade because butchering is such a "brutal and odious business." Rees points out that if enough workers do not find butchering unpleasant, "it would then clearly be possible to fill all positions for butchers without any compensating wage differential" (Killingsworth 1985a:96). Thus, the market-determined compensating wage differential for the unpleasantness of butchering depends not on Adam Smith's tastes but on the preferences of the *marginal* recruit into the butchering trade.

If in fact anyone attempted to value (or weigh) job traits based on Adam Smith's or anyone else's *a priori* judgments, this would be a valid criticism of the analysis. But in practice job evaluations typically use market wages to fix a dollar value to their factor points, at least for benchmark jobs, as discussed in Chapter 2. In this approach job traits are only *measured,* not valued, by job analysts. Thus, comparable worth does not demand, as critics have charged, that heretofore uncompensated traits should be rewarded according to the judgment of some group of experts, but only that men's and women's jobs should pay the same return on any given trait. In our own work presented below, job analysts' judgments determine what, for example, different jobs' skill levels are, but market wage rates are used to impute values (or returns) to those skill levels. Thus our equations should reflect the marginal worker's and firm's valuation of all job and worker traits.

ALTERNATIVE MODELS OF COMPARABLE WORTH

In neoclassical economics jobs do not exist, or alternatively, each worker's job is unique. Productivity is embodied in the *worker* (acquired through worker investment in human capital) and wages are a function of the worker's productivity. In actual practice wage rates (or at least base rates) are typically assigned to jobs, not individuals in the abstract. *Jobs* are evaluated and rated according their traits or requirements, and wages are set accordingly—usually with an adjustment for the employee's length of service and relevant work experience or training. Wages are based on some notion of productivity, but productivity is viewed primarily an attribute of the job, rather than the person who holds it.

AN ADVOCATE'S MODEL OF COMPARABLE WORTH

The perception that wages are attributable to jobs, not individuals, has led virtually all studies of comparable worth to focus on job or occupational wages. A common approach is to estimate separate wage equations for "women's jobs" (or female-dominated jobs) and for "men's jobs" or for women's jobs versus all other jobs. Occupational wages are regressed on a variety of traits that are common to all jobs. These may be traits that adhere to the job, such as working conditions, or they may be embodied in the workers in those jobs, such as their level of education. In the latter case it is assumed that the average level of education of workers in a particular job reflects the job's educational requirements. Wages in women's jobs are then adjusted using the equation estimated for men's jobs or for all nonfemale-dominated jobs.

Our advocate's model follows these procedures closely. We employ the NLS and DOT data described in Chapter 3. We estimate four separate equations: one for men's jobs (occupations employing at least 80 percent men), another for women's jobs (occupations employing at least 70 percent women), another for all jobs other than women's jobs, and finally one for all jobs. The cutoff is lower for women than for men because they comprise less than half the labor force. The 70 percent cutoff for women's jobs is commonly used in published empirical work on occupa-

Table 4–1. Means of Variables.

Variable	All Jobs	Female- Dominated Jobs	Nonfemale- Dominated Jobs	Male- Dominated Jobs
WAGE	$7.04	$5.56	$7.77	$8.23
PFEM	.437	.867	.223	.055
PBLK	.255	.273	.247	.236
SCH	13.14	13.16	13.13	12.76
XPR	5.02	4.47	5.30	5.88
TEN	5.81	5.23	6.10	6.19
GED	11.68	11.72	11.67	11.61
SVP	1.86	1.17	2.21	2.46
GOVT	.224	.281	.196	.157
CBRG	.360	.276	.402	.399
CORE	.174	.093	.215	.211
PERF	.255	.122	.322	.407
SO	.429	.429	.428	.447
SMSA	.697	.706	.693	.690
N (individuals)	3,297	1,096	2,201	1,121

Note: Variables are defined in Table 3–3. Female-dominated jobs are occupations that are 70 percent or more female; male-dominated jobs are 80 percent or more male. Nonfemale jobs are all occupations except those that are female-dominated.

tional segregation and comparable worth, and the 80 percent cutoff for men's jobs represents a corresponding disproportionality of men.[3]

In each of these equations, average wages for occupation i $(\overline{W}_i)$ are a function of six *job traits*, $\overline{T}_{ij}$ (the average level of trait j in occupation i), and six industry and location control variables, $\overline{C}_{ij}$ (the average level of control j in occupation i). These variables are defined in Table 3–3. Their means for each set of jobs are presented in Table 4–1.

The full model is then

$$\overline{W}_i = a + \Sigma_j\, b_j\overline{T}_{ij} + \Sigma_j\, c_j\overline{C}_{ij}$$

where the b_j and c_j represent the net return to job traits (traits both of the job itself and of the workers in it) and to the industry and regional controls, respectively. For example, the coefficient on GED would give us the (compensating) wage differential between two occupations that differ in their average general educational development requirement by one year, holding all other traits constant.[4] The remaining industry and location control variables are added to control for variations in occupational wages that would not be affected by a comparable worth law that applied at the level of the individual employer (which we assume is typically situated in a single industry and area).

The regression of occupational wages on average job traits estimates the market-clearing compensating wage differential for each trait (the b_j), and the principle of comparable worth is violated by the existence of different compensating differentials for the same job traits in men's and women's jobs. Regression results are contained in Table 4–2 below. We note briefly that women's jobs appear to pay *higher* returns to schooling, experience, and job tenure than do men's jobs. The advantage to men's jobs is (once again) all in the constant term. We note also that women's jobs are also the only ones in which the percentage of black workers in the occupation does not have a large negative impact.

These results can be employed to partition the wage gap between women's jobs and other jobs into a portion due to differences in levels of explanatory variables, a portion due to differences in constant terms, and a portion due to differences in coefficients or returns to the variables, as described in Appendix 2–C. The results of this partitioning between women's jobs and other (or nonfemale-dominated) jobs are presented in Table 4–3. The partitioning attributes 49 percent of the wage gap ($1.08 of a total gap of $2.22) between female-dominated and other jobs to differences in *levels* of job (and worker) traits. On the question of *returns* to the job traits we find that the wage gap would be *increased* by $5.06 if workers in women's jobs were paid the same returns as workers in other jobs. It is the differences in constant terms ($4.73) and in levels and returns to industry and location controls that bestow the advantage to workers in nonfemale-dominated jobs and that "account" for most of the difference in wages between women's and other jobs.[5]

The usual comparable worth wage formula simply uses the constant term and job trait coefficients for other jobs to adjust wages in women's jobs. This approach yields an average wage adjustment of $.63, an 11.3 percent increase in the wages of workers in women's jobs, and a 28.4 percent reduction in the wage gap between those workers and all others.

Table 4–2. Occupational Wage Equations: Advocate's Model (Dependent Variable: Mean Wages in the Occupation).

Variable	All Jobs	Female-Dominated Jobs	Nonfemale-Dominated Jobs	Male-Dominated Jobs
CONST(WT)	−10.174[b]	−11.781[b]	−7.052[b]	−4.189
PBLK	−1.842[b]	.649	−3.052[b]	−2.207[a]
SCH	.721[b]	.921[b]	.528[b]	.402[a]
XPR	.573[b]	.380[a]	.481[b]	.223[a]
TEN	.507[b]	.284[b]	.408[b]	.225[a]
GED	−.094	.041	.016	.230
SVP	.399[b]	−.013	.258[b]	.057
GOVT	−.794[a]	−2.605[b]	−.287	−.389
CBRG	.793[a]	1.505[a]	.194	.996
CORE	1.404[b]	1.560[a]	1.653[b]	1.480[a]
PERF	1.117[b]	−.527	1.502[b]	1.543[b]
SO	.099	.751	−.131	−.964
SMSA	2.951[b]	1.847[a]	2.971[b]	2.097[a]
N (occupations)	219	49	170	116

a. Denotes significance at the .05 level.
b. Denotes significance at the .01 level.
Note: Variables are defined in Table 3–3. For a definition of the job categories see the note to Table 4–1. Equations are estimated using the weighted least squares procedure described in Chapter 3 (see especially note 4 in Chapter 3).

We calculate the effect this would have on the overall male/female earnings gap by noting that 65.9 percent of the women and 7.9 percent of the men in the sample are in female-dominated jobs, and all of these workers receive an average wage increase of $.63. Averaging in other workers whose wages remain unchanged yields an average wage increase of .659($.63) = $.42 for women and .079($.63) = $.05 for men, reducing the male/female wage gap of $3.03 by $.37 or 12.1 percent.

CRITIQUE OF THE ADVOCATE'S MODEL

The advocate's wage adjustment formula follows the "equal pay for comparable *jobs*" interpretation of comparable worth. We have already shown that this interpretation (as opposed to the "equal returns to job traits" formulation) cannot be defended

Table 4–3. Partitioning the Occupational
Wage Gap: Advocate's Model.

Variable Group	Amount of Difference That Is Due to:		
	Levels	*Returns*	*Total*
Constant	—	$4.73	$4.73
Job traits	$1.08	− $5.06	− $3.98
Industry and location controls	$0.51	$0.96	$1.47
Total	$1.59	$.63	$2.22

Source: Computed from data in Tables 4–1 and 4–2 by procedures described in the text.

from critics charges that it assumes that the whole differences in constant terms is due to discrimination, thereby ignoring important, economically valid causes of wage differentials between jobs.

Empirically, this procedure is illegitimate because in including the constant term in the wage adjustment it eliminates differences in occupational wages that result from causes other than an occupation's "femaleness." Moreover, since our sample compares wages across firms, interfirm differences in sex composition of occupations and wages that are not captured by our industry and location controls are also contained in the constant term.[6] In fact, comparable worth implemented on a firm-by-firm basis would have no impact on these differences, but a procedure that equates constant terms implies otherwise.

Thus, any procedure that attempts to assess the impact of comparable worth cannot legitimately assume that eliminating the effect of the "femaleness" of an occupation on its wages would equalize the constant terms in regression equations such as those above. But as Table 4–3 shows, if we "correct" only for differences in the coefficients of our job trait variables, we would actually *increase* the wage gap between female-dominated and other jobs by $5.06! Clearly, this is implausible. A substantial part of the difference in constant terms almost certainly needs to be in our wage adjustment.[7] But how much?

Even without all of these difficulties, there are problems

created by the arbitrary definition of "female job" (70 percent or more women in the occupation). First, there is the problem that this is a completely arbitrary cutoff. There is no rationale for the 70 percent cutoff or for denying workers in slightly less female jobs any adjustment. For example, using our cutoff, the Census occupation "speech therapists," which is 74 percent female, would receive a comparable worth wage adjustment, but "therapists not elsewhere classified," which is 68 percent female, would not. In effect, women who have managed to enter a slightly less traditionally female occupation would be penalized for their efforts. Table 4–4 lists some major female-employing occupations that fall under the 70 percent cutoff.

And consider how such a comparable worth adjustment

Table 4–4. Almost Women's Work: Selected Occupations That Would Not Qualify under a 70 Percent Cutoff.

Occupation	Number of Women	Percentage of Women Workers	Percent Female	Female Wage
Therapists not elsewhere classified	18,211	.04	68.0	$5.59
Teachers, special education	10,138	.02	69.1	5.94
Teachers, not elsewhere classified	126,047	.28		
Recreation workers	12,122	.03	67.6	4.31
Social workers	161,258	.36	64.9	6.32
Health technicians not elsewhere classified	55,858	.13	63.4	5.06
Hotel clerks	21,113	.05	68.2	3.70
Cost and rate clerk	27,725	.06	68.8	5.14
Laundry and dry clean operators	65,388	.15	65.0	3.62
Hand packers and packagers	206,834	.47	66.8	4.60

Source: U.S. Bureau of the Census (1984a, 1984b).

might work within a single private firm. Such a cutoff will create strong incentives to hold the proportion of women in each occupation below the magic number of 70 percent. This could not help but affect hiring and transfer policies and will, in effect, raise the premium on discrimination. Men might be actively recruited for jobs that are just over any arbitrary cutoff, while women will be discouraged from entering jobs that are just below that cutoff. As Johnson and Solon (1984:11n) suggest, highly "feminized" jobs might even be contracted out to other firms to avoid comparable worth comparisons. That such evasive practices on the part of employers may be illegal does not mean that they would not occur.

We now turn to an alternative formulation of how comparable worth would correct for discrimination against workers in female-dominated jobs, which we believe is faithful to the principles of comparable worth, is more consistent with standard economic theory, and avoids the inequity of an arbitrary dividing line between "female jobs" (whose wages are adjusted) and "other jobs" (whose wages are not adjusted).

AN ECONOMIST'S MODEL

In Chapter 3 we argued that the demand for comparable worth derives from a perception that occupational segregation results in the "devaluing" of women's jobs. Perhaps because of employer prejudices (based on cultural stereotypes) jobs are perceived to have "genders" and an occupation's gender affects its wages and returns to job traits. In the first section of this chapter, we argued that one can interpret comparable worth as an effort to do what an efficient, nondiscriminating labor market should do: make compensating wage differentials between occupations (that is, returns to job traits in different occupations) independent of the sex composition of those occupations. Thus, to estimate the effects of comparable worth on wages in women's jobs, we need a variable that captures the wage differential between occupations resulting from differences in their gender or level of femaleness. The obvious choice is the percentage of workers in the occupation who are female.

Consider two jobs, one that has a below-average number of women workers and the other that has more than the average number of women. Suppose for simplicity of exposition that wages in these jobs depend on their gender and on one general-ized job trait T. Comparable worth advocates argue that women's jobs pay low wages because women's work is under-valued. This implies that the higher the percentage of women in an occupation, the less all workers in the occupation are paid and possibly the lower their returns to job trait T. Thus we esti-mate separately for men and women the same equation that we used to obtain our best estimate of the effects of occupational segregation—viz., equation (3.4) in Chapter 3:

$$\overline{W}_i^s = a^s + b^s F_i + \Sigma_j c_j^s \overline{T}_{ij}^s + \Sigma_j d_j^s \overline{C}_{ij}^s + \Sigma_j g_j^s F_i \overline{T}_{ij}^s + \Sigma_j h_j^s F_i \overline{C}_{ij}^s \tag{4.1}$$

where $\overline{W}_i^s$ is the mean wage for sex s in occupation i,
          F_i is the percent female in the occupation i,
          $\overline{T}_{ij}^s$ is the mean level of job/worker trait j for sex s in occupation i, and
          $\overline{C}_{ij}^s$ is the mean level of industry/regional control j for sex s in occupation i.

The rationale for this specification is that by interacting all job traits and control variables with percent female in the occupation we isolate all wage effects (both direct and indirect) that are specifically associated with an occupation's gender. We eliminate these effects by setting $b^s = g_j^s = h_j^s = 0$ in both the men's and the women's equations.[8] Our comparable worth wage adjustment, then entails subtracting

$$cwa^m = b^m F_i + e_j^m F_i \overline{T}_{ij}^m + f_j^m F_i \overline{C}_{ij}^m \tag{4.2}$$

from the wages of men in occupation i and either

$$cwa_1^f = b^f F_i + g_i^f F_i \overline{T}_{ij}^f + h_j^f F_i \overline{C}_{ij}^f \tag{4.3}$$

or

$$cwa_2^f = b^m F_i + g_i^m F_i \overline{T}_{ij}^f + h_j^m F_i \overline{C}_{ij}^f \tag{4.4}$$

from the wages of women in occupation i.

Equations (4.2) to (4.4) adjust men's and women's wages for the effects of percent female on their respective occupational wages. A simplified example of this adjustment process is shown in Figure 4–3 where we ignore the interaction terms in the above equations and show occupational wages of both men and women declining linearly with percent female. The comparable worth wage adjustment that eliminates the effect of percent female on the wages of the typical male worker (that is, the adjustment obtained from plugging $F_i = .224$ into equation (4.2) is shown by the vertical distance AB. The adjustment that eliminates the effect of percent female on the wages of the typical female worker is shown by the vertical distance DE. In this illustration men in any given occupation get a bigger wage adjustment than women in that occupation do. But they get a smaller overall average adjustment than women because the average man is in a much less female-dominated occupation (22.4 percent versus 71.2 percent).

But why are the comparable worth adjustment lines *different* for men and women? They are different because we used the female occupational wage structure to estimate the effect of percent female on women's wages and the male occupational wage structure to estimate the effect of percent female on men's wages.[9] And why is the "per unit" penalty *greater* for men than women? Our theoretical discussion in Chapter 3 suggested a model of discrimination in which *intra*occupational wage differentials between men and women were the greatest in those occupations in which women were the most completely excluded. That is, occupational segregation depresses women's wages (relative to men's) most in male-dominated occupations and least in female-dominated occupations. Likewise, it *raises* men's wages most (relative to women's) in the most male-dominated occupations and raises them least (again, relative to women's) in female-dominated jobs.

Since most women are in relatively female-dominated occupations and most men are in relatively male-dominated occupations, our estimates of the effect of percent female on men's and women's occupational wages understate the total (inter- and intraoccupational) effect of occupational segregation on women's wages and overstate the total effect on men's wages. We therefore view equation (4.3) as a likely underestimate—or lower-bound estimate—of the appropriate adjustment for women. In contrast, equation (4.4), using the estimated coefficients from the male occupational earnings equation, provides an alternative upper-bound estimate of the comparable worth wage adjustment

Figure 4–3. Effect of Percent Female in an Occupation on Men's and Women's Wages in the Occupation.

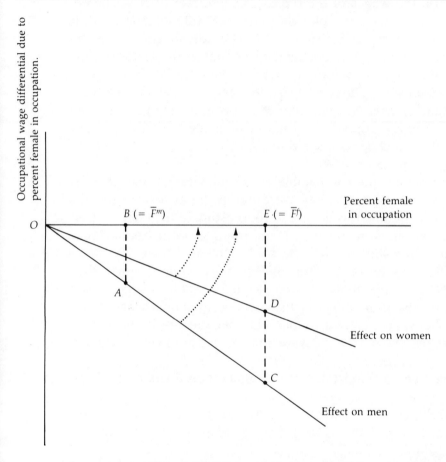

for women. This adjustment is represented by the vertical distance *CE* in Figure 4–3.

Table 4–5, Part A, presents the average wage adjustments based on these formulas for men (using equation (4.2) and for women (lower-bound using equation (4.3) and upper-bound using equation (4.4), each evaluated at the sample mean for women). Using separate equations for men and women, we find that comparable worth applied to all jobs raises men's wages by $.20 (or 2.5 percent) and women's by $.29 (or 5.4 percent). Since men's wages are increased almost as much as women's, the

Table 4–5. Comparable Worth Wage Adjustments.

Group	Initial Wage	Comparable Worth Adjustment		Adjusted Wage
		$	%	
A. All workers (N = 3,297, 43.7% female)				
Men	$8.36	$.20	2.5%	$8.56
Women				
Lower estimate	5.33	.29	5.4	5.62
Upper estimate	5.33	.73	13.8	6.06
Total				
Lower estimate	7.04	.24	3.4	7.28
Upper estimate	7.04	.44	6.2	7.47
B. Workers in Female Dominated Occupations (N = 1,096, 86.7% female)				
Men	$7.80	$.38	4.9%	$8.18
Women				
Lower estimate	5.21	.34	6.6	5.56
Upper estimate	5.21	.81	15.6	6.02
Total				
Lower estimate	5.56	.35	6.3	5.91
Upper estimate	5.56	.75	13.6	6.31

Note: Calculations based on equations (4.2) to (4.4) in text. Rows may not add exactly due to rounding.

male/female wage gap is reduced by only $.09 (or 2.8 percent). Alternatively, if we use the men's equation to estimate the women's wage adjustment (our upper-bound estimate based on equation (4.4)), women's wages increase by $.73 (or 13.8 percent), and the wage gap is reduced by $.53 (or 17.4 percent).

Part B of Table 4–5 presents the same adjustments for workers in occupations that are 70 percent or more female. Here the effects are larger because we are focusing on workers in the most female-dominated occupations. And the average adjustment based on equations (4.2 and 4.3) is actually slightly larger for men than for women in absolute terms ($.38 versus $.34). However, if we use equation (4.4) we get an upper-bound estimate for women in female-dominated jobs of $.81 (or 15.6 percent). Finally, we get lower and upper bound adjustments for all workers in female-dominated jobs of $.35 and $.75, respecitvely. These estimates can be compared with a comparable worth wage adjustment of $.63 (or 11.3 percent) for all workers in female-dominated jobs under the advocate's model. The upper-bound estimate given by the economist's approach thus yields results that are similar to those of the advocate's model (in terms of their overall impact on wages in female-dominated jobs) and to actual practice, where comparable worth studies in state and local governments have found that "women's jobs" are underpaid by between 10 and 20 percent.

DO WOMEN CHOOSE LOWER-PAYING JOBS?

As we noted in Chapter 3, a number of economists have argued that male/female occupational distributions reflect differences between men and women in job preferences and choices (Polachek 1979, 1981; Filer 1983; Killingworth 1985a). While this argument takes various forms, a typical rendition goes something like this: Most women have different job preferences than men. Because they expect to drop out of the labor force to bear and rear children, some women may choose jobs with little potential for training and wage growth. Also, women are socialized from childhood to prefer "pink-collar" clerical jobs and nursing and teaching professions that they believe are appropriate to their sex.

In this view differences between men's and women's occupational distributions simply reflect differences in their job preferences. If this were so, then the percent female variable in our equations would be acting as a proxy for some qualities of the job that make it more attractive to women than to men. And this would invalidate our whole analysis, since we would be "correcting" for a valid compensating wage differential—the lower wage that workers (mostly women) are willing to accept for the more desirable working conditions in female-dominated occupations.

Although systematic differences in preferences may account for some difference in men's and women's occupational distributions, they should not cause differential returns to job traits. Thus, while this argument may rationalize a negative coefficient on percent female in our wage equations, it does not justify *different* coefficients for men and women, as long as the relationship between job traits and wages is linear. But if the relationship between wage rates and some working condition such as risk of injury is nonlinear, it ought to be concave with higher risk levels yielding diminishing returns.[10] If percent female were simply a proxy for (say) low risk, our findings, with men paying a relatively high penalty for percent female and being in relatively low percent female jobs, would in fact imply a convex relationship between wages and risk, which is theoretically untenable. We conclude that the differential returns to percent female are unlikely to reflect a single wage-working-conditions function.[11]

There is some evidence that differences in working conditions between typical male and female jobs do account for part of the wage gap. Filer (1985), for example, finds statistically significant differences between men and women on ten of twenty-four different self-reported job characteristics. When he adds all twenty-four of these variables to a standard human capital wage equation the adjusted R^2 increases from .36 to .41 for men and .35 to .47 for women. More importantly, these working conditions variables increase the portion of the wage gap between men and women explained by differences in levels of the independent variables (evaluated using the coefficients from the male equation) from 48.3 percent to 65.5 percent.[12]

To evaluate this challenge to our analysis of the effect of an occupation's gender on its wages we utilize a comprehensive set of job characteristics data provided by the *Dictionary of Occupational Title* or *DOT* (exhaustively described and analyzed in Miller et al. 1980). The *DOT* job descriptions have been mapped into the Census occupation codes used by the NLS by the Center for Human Resources at Ohio State University, providing us with forty-nine variables measuring all manner of job requirements and working conditions. A factor analysis of these data reduces them to three underlying components or factors that accounted for over 60 percent of the variance in the original variables. These factors were interpreted (based on their factor loadings) to represent each occupation's intellectual demands *(INTL)*, physical demands and working conditions *(PHYS)*, and interpersonal demands *(PSNL)*. Each occupation's factor scores on these three factors provide our three new job characteristics variables. These variables are arbitrarily scaled (with zero mean and unit standard deviation) and were eventually dropped from our main analysis due to the problems arising with the use of arbitrarily scaled variables discussed in Chapters 2 and 3. Nevertheless, they provide a comprehensive set of job characteristics indicators that can be used here to evaluate the argument that our percent female variable really reflects differences in occupations' working conditions and worker preferences, rather than simply their "gender."

The simple correlations presented in Part A of Table 4–6 reveal a negative association between percent female in an occupation and these three job characteristics variables, most important, between percent female and the physical demands and working conditions of the job. In five out of six instances this negative correlation holds within each job group as well. Moreover, as we see in Part B of this table, the difference between female-dominated and other occupations in their levels on all of these variables is substantial and statistically significant.

To see if percent female is simply acting as a proxy for working conditions rather than as an indication of a job's gender, we purged our percent female variable of all variance shared with these working conditions variables and reestimated equation (3.3) for men and women.[13] The result (shown in Part C of Table 4–6) is that the negative effect of PFEM on men's occupational wages remains virtually unchanged, and the negative effect of percent female on women's occupational wages declines by two-fifths.

While these results do not permit us decisively to set aside the objection that *PFEM* is really measuring relevant (positive) job characteristics, they still favor a comparable worth interpretation of the role of percent female on occupational wages over a "legitimate compensating wage differential" interpretation. They do indicate that the absence of job characteristics measures from our equations has a substantial effect on our estimate of the effect of percent female on women's, but not men's, wages. We conclude then that our lower-bound estimates (based on equation (4.3)) of the effect of an occupation's gender on the wages it pays may overstate the true effect by two-thirds ((1/.6)–1). But the upperbound estimates (based on equation (4.4)) remain unchanged.

Table 4–6. The Relationship between Percent Female in an Occupation and Undesirable Working Conditions.

A. Correlation with Percent Female

Variables	All Occupations	Female-Dominated Occupations	Other Occupations
INTL	−.189	.200	−.085
PHYS	−.705	−.217	−.226
PSNL	−.024	−.460	−.618

B. Means (Standard Deviations)

Variables	Female-Dominated Occupations	Other Occupations	Difference
INTL	−.257 (.875)	.029 (1.076)	.286[a]
PHYS	−.806 (.689)	.404 (.939)	1.210[a]
PSNL	−.293 (.921)	−.034 (1.009)	.259[a]

C. Effect on Coefficient of Percent Female in Wage Equation

	Men	Women
PFEM	−.686	−.586
PFEMR	−.696	−.348

a. Denotes that the difference is significant at the .01 level.

Note: The coefficients of PFEM are from equation (3) in Tables 3–5a and 3–5b. The coefficients of PFEMR are from the same equations with all variance that PFEM shares with INTL, PHYS, and PSNL removed from PFEM.

CONCLUSION

We find that comparable worth as we have specified it in our economist's model would raise earnings in women's jobs by between 4 percent and 14 percent, suggesting a ballpark estimate on the order of 10 percent. The obvious questions are whether this is a lot or a little and whether the figures are indicative of what we should expect to find in real life.

Size is a relative matter, and raising earnings in women's jobs by 10 percent would be no small achievement. Most studies of the impact of unionization suggest that on the average unions raise wages by 10 to 15 percent (Freeman and Medoff 1984). No federal labor policy that we know of has had this much affect on wages in women's jobs since the NRA codes and minimum wage legislation of the 1930s.

Still, we suspect that most supporters of comparable worth would think that wage increases on the order of 10 percent are quite small, while its business opponents would be greatly relieved if that were all it would cost them. In fact, however— despite our radically different specification of the comparable worth wage correction—our upper-bound estimates are remarkably close to estimates obtained from our advocate's model and to the 10 to 20 percent wage adjustments recommended in comparable worth studies in Los Angeles, San Jose, the state of Washington, and elsewhere.

The other important differences between our analysis and "real life" comparable worth studies—besides the differences in our models of comparable worth—is that our data are national, while comparable worth has actually been implemented at the level of the individual employer. Since some of the male/female differences in our data are due to *interindustry* and *interfirm* differences in wages and percent female (see note 6), our estimates *overstate* the dollar impact that this approach would be likely to have at the level of the individual employer.

In this chapter we have shown that the advocate's model of comparable worth is flawed for precisely the same reasons that the real-life applications of comparable worth critiqued in Chapter 2 are flawed. Even though there is a reasonable presumption that some part of the difference in constant terms in the occupational wage equations for women's and other jobs stems from discriminatory devaluation of women's work, there are other valid explanations for this difference. As a result, these methods actually adjust for more than what comparable worth supporters claim to be seeking to correct. Moreover, we have shown that economic theory cannot support the advocate's formulation.

Our alternative economist's approach is consistent with standard economic theory and with the claim that it raises wages in women's jobs by the amount that they are depressed by occupational segregation. We believe that our findings provide the best estimates so far of the impact of an economically meaningful comparable worth wage adjustment on the occupational wage structure and the male/female wage gap.

We note that these estimates—although based on a different model of comparable worth—are quite similar in magnitude to the wage adjustments actually made where comparable worth has been implemented. In one sense our results therefore serve to vindicate real-life comparable worth wage settlements. Nevertheless, we conclude that current approaches to comparable worth are inconsistent with the basic principles of the market economy. While this may not weigh heavily on the minds of many advocates of comparable worth, it should be recognized as a serious *political* liability in a society where the free market ideology is as strong as it is in the United States. The alternative model presented in this chapter therefore should serve not only to advance the economic case for comparable worth, but also possibly its political viability.

NOTES

1. This conclusion holds as long as returns to training are linear (that is, constant returns), as the straight-line $W(T)$ in Figure 3–1 implies. Only if returns are nonlinear and if two jobs are very different in terms of their training requirements will their returns to training differ significantly. In terms of men's and women's jobs, only if men's jobs require much more training and if there are *increasing* returns to training would training pay higher returns in men's jobs than in women's jobs. In fact, there do not seem to be any relevant jobs traits for which these two necessary conditions for nondiscriminatory unequal returns hold, and the literature on compensating wage differentials generally assumes decreasing, rather than increasing, returns.

2. As Smith (1979) shows in the case of assessing the value of risk abatement, using the slope of $W(T_j)$ to estimate the value of a nonmarginal reduction of risk in a job *overstates* the benefit to workers in that job because the slope of $W(T_j)$ is greater than the slope of the workers' indifference curve to the left of any point of tangency between these two curves. Analogously, the slope of $W(T_j)$ *understates* the value to employers of a worker who performs a job with a given level of risk because the slope of $W(T_j)$ is less than the slope of the employer's iso-profit curve to the left of their tangency.

3. These criteria for male- and female-dominated jobs were derived as follows: In 1980 civilian nonagricultural employment was 43.2 percent female. An occupation in which women were represented in proportion to their numbers in total employment would therefore employee 432 women for every 1,000 employees or 432 women for every 568 men. If women are *overrepresented* by a factor of three, there would be $3 \times 432 = 1,296$ women for every 568 men—that is, the occupation would be $1,296/(1,296 + 568) = 70$ percent female. Likewise, an occupation in which men were overrepresented by a factor of three would contain $3 \times 568 = 1,704$ men for every 432 women—that is, it would be $1,704/(1,704 + 432) = 80$ percent male.

4. This interpretation depends on the assumption that there are enough different kinds of jobs so that it is always possible to find two jobs that are equivalent in terms of all but one of their traits. In this case mobile workers can, by changing jobs, adjust the level of each job trait holding constant the levels of the others, and our estimates of the returns to each trait are independent of the levels of and returns to others. This is a common assumption in the analysis of compensating wage differentials.

5. A similar partitioning is performed in Buchele and Aldrich (1985) with quite dissimiliar results. We attribute the differences in results to differences in the earnings models and estimating procedures employed in that study versus the present one.

6. Blau (1975) has shown interfirm differences in the sex composition of clerical occupations to be an important cause of male/female earnings difference in these occupations. Also see Treiman and Hartmann (1981:39–40).

7. Finally, we recall the problem raised in our discussion of Ehrenberg and Smith's (1984) analysis of the state of Minnesota's job evaluation data (Chapter 2). There we argued that no meaningful partitioning of the wage gap between differences due to coefficients and those due to constant terms is possible when the wage equations contain arbitrarily scaled variables. Although this particular problem is not an issue in our analysis (precisely because we have avoided using such arbitrarily scaled variables), it is frequently a problem in other analyses, such as those using Hay points, Willis points, and factor scores (as Treiman, Hartmann, and Roos 1984 do, for example).

8. Note the difference between this adjustment and our estimate of the effect of occupational segregation in Chapter 3. There we set F_i equal to the sample mean to measure the effect of moving women out of female-dominated occupations and men out of male-dominated occupations until men and women were represented in each occupation in proportion to their numbers in the whole sample. Here we eliminate the effect on occupational wages of the sexual composition of occupations by setting the coefficients of all terms containing F_i equal to zero. This interpretation of a comparable worth wage adjustment (without the indirect or interaction effects) is also used by Johnson and Solon (1984).

9. This was necessary because if we had used the mean occupational wages of all workers (that is, both men and women) our percent female variable would simply be picking up the fact that women's wages are generally lower than men's (the weighted average effect described in our critique of the Treiman, Hartmann, and Roos (1984) study in Chapter 3).

10. A concave curve is one whose slope (in this case the compensating wage differential associated with risk) declines as the independent variable increases. Compensating wage differential analysis postulates a concave envelope of market clearing equilibrium wage differentials due to the presence of risk-seeking individuals and rising costs per unit of risk reduction undertaken by employers.

11. Filer (1985:432) finds that adding quadratic terms to his earnings equations does not significantly increase their explanatory power and notes that this implies that the coefficients of his linear equations are "due to a difference between the sexes in the terms of trade between working conditions rather than to men and women being at different places on a common nonlinear wage locus."
12. On the other hand, other empirical research has been largely unsuccessful in finding compensating wage differentials for any working conditions or job characteristics other than death risk. See, for example, Brown's (1980) estimates and review of previous research and Barry (1985) for evidence that men, but not women, receive compensating differentials for hazardous work.
13. This was done by regressing *PFEM* on *INTL*, *PHYS*, and *PSNL* and using the residuals from this regression (which we name *PFEMR)* in place of *PFEM* in the wage equations. The coefficient on our "purged" variable indicates the effect of percent female on occupational wages *net* of any effect shared with these working conditions variables. (This, of course, has the same effect on the coefficient of *PFEM* as merely including these two variables in the original equation.) In any case, we note that this test is "conservative" in that it attributes all explanatory power that *PFEM* shares with the job characteristics to the latter. This procedure therefore gives an upper-bound estimate of the extent to which the absence of these job characteristics variables from our model vitiates our results.

BIBLIOGRAPHY

Barry, Janis. 1985. "Women Production Workers: Low Pay and Hazardous Work." *The American Economics Review* 75 (May):262–65.
Blau, Francine. 1975. "Sex Segregation of Workers by Enterprise in Clerical Occupations." In *Labor Market Segmentation,* edited by R. Edwards, M. Reich, and D. Gordon, pp. 257–78. Lexington, Mass.: D. C. Heath.
Buchele, Robert, and Mark Aldrich. 1985. "How Much Difference Would Comparable Worth Make?" *Industrial Relations* 24 (Spring):222–33.
Brown, Charles. 1980. "Equalizing Differences in the Labor Market." *The Quarterly Journal of Economics* 94 (Feb.):113–34.
Bunzel, John. 1982. "To Each According to Her Worth?" *Public Interest* 67 (Spring):77–93.
Ehrenberg, Ronald, and Robert Smith. 1984. "Comparable Worth in the Public Sector." *Working Paper* No. 1471. Cambridge, Mass.: National Bureau Economic Research.
Filer, Randall K. 1983. "Sexual Differences in Earnings: The Role of Individual Personalities and Tastes." *The Journal of Human Resources* 18 (Winter):82 –99.
_____. 1985. "Male–Female Wage Differences: The Importance of Compensating Differentials." *Industrial and Labor Relations Review* 38 (April):426–37.
Freeman, Richard, and James Medoff. 1984. *What Do Unions Do? New York: Basic Books.*
Johnson, George, and Gary Solon. 1984. "Pay Differences between Women's and Men's Jobs: The Empirical Foundations of Comparable Worth Legislation." National Bureau of Economic Research Working Paper No. 1472.

Killingsworth, Mark R. 1985a. "Economic Analysis of Comparable Worth and Its Consequences." Paper presented at the 37th Annual Meeting of the Industrial Relations Research Association, Dallas, Texas (Dec. 28–30, 1984:183–89).

_____. 1985b. "The Economics of Comparable Worth: Analytical, Empirical, and Policy Questions." In *Comparable Worth: New Directions for Research*, edited by Heidi Hartmann, pp. 86–115. Washington, D.C.: National Academy Press.

Miller, A.; D. Treiman; P. Cain; and P. Roos, eds. 1980. *Work, Jobs, and Occupations: A Critical Review of the Dictionary of Occupational Titles*. Washington, D.C.: National Academy Press.

New York Times. 1982–1985.

Polachek, Solomon. 1979. "Occupational Segregation among Women: Theory, Evidence, and a Prognosis." In *Women in the Labor Market*, edited by Cynthia B. Lloyd, pp. 137–57. New York: Columbia University Press.

_____. 1981. "Occupational Self-Selection: A Human Capital Approach to Sex Differences in Occupational Structure." *Review of Economics and Statistics* (Feb.):60–69.

Remick, Helen. 1985. "Major Issues in *A Priori* Applications." In *Comparable Worth and Wage Discrimination: Technical Possibilities and Political Realities*, edited by Helen Remick, pp. 99–117. Philadelphia: Temple University Press.

Smith, Robert S. 1979. "Compensating Wage Differentials and Public Policy: A Review." *Industrial and Labor Relations Review* 32 (April):339–52.

Thaler, Richard, and Sherwin Rosen. 1975. "The Value of Saving a Life: Evidence from the Labor Market." In *Household Production and Consumption*, edited by Nestor Terleckyj, pp. 265–301. New York: National Bureau of Economic Research.

Treiman, Donald and Heidi Hartmann. 1981. "Women, Work and Wages." Washington, D.C.: National Academy Press.

Treiman, D., H. Hartmann, and P. Roos. 1984. "Assessing Pay Discrimination Using National Data." In *Comparable Worth and Wage Discrimination*, edited by Helen Remick, pp. 137–154. Philadelphia: Temple University Press.

U.S. Bureau of the Census. 1984a. 1980 Census of Population. *Detailed Occupation of the Experienced Civilian Labor Force by Sex for the United States and Regions: 1970 and 1980*. Washington, D.C.: GPO.

_____. 1984b. 1980 Census of Population. *Earnings by Occupation and Education*. Washington, D.C.: GPO.

Washington Post. 1982–1985.

CHAPTER 5

The Distributional Impact of Comparable Worth

The maintenance man would be paid less so the librarian could be paid more.
-MICHAEL J. HOROWITZ, U.S. Office of Management and Budget *(New York Times, Sept. 4, 1984:B8)*

What you are really talking about is a scheme for redistributing the wealth in this country.
-LINDA CHAVEZ, staff director of the U.S. Commission on Civil Rights *(Washington Post, April 5, 1985:2)*

INTRODUCTION

Critics of the feminist movement of the 1970s have charged that its constituency was largely white, middle-class women. Opponents of the comparable worth movement have followed suit, with Clarence Pendelton characterizing comparable worth as "reparations for middle-class white women" *(Washington Post, 1985:2)* and Michael Horowitz arguing that it would "help middle class white women at the expense of blacks *(Comparable Worth Project Newsletter 1985:2).* Conservative opponents of comparable worth thus perceive it as elitist and inimical to the interests of "working people" and nonwhites. While this criticism is obviously highly rhetorical, our review in Chapter 2 of job evaluation did suggest that job rating systems may "devalue" blue-collar jobs, perhaps especially those held by blacks. Moreover, the issue is politically important. For if the comparable worth movement is really as divisive and narrowly based in the special interests of the relatively well-to-do as its opponents claim, it is not likely to win the kind of broad-based political support it seeks.

Thus, the argument that comparable worth would disproportionately benefit white, relatively well-paid workers deserves a hearing. In this chapter we investigate the likely impact of comparable worth on specific occupations and occupational classes: on public versus private-sector workers, on the relative earnings of blacks and whites, and on the overall distribution of income.

WOMEN'S JOBS AND WOMEN'S EARNINGS

We begin with a simple survey of the jobs in which women are concentrated and of their average earnings. While such data cannot tell us conclusively whether comparable worth is as middle class as the critics charge, they provide a good starting point and a check on our subsequent analysis.

AN OVERVIEW

Appendix 5–A contains U.S. Census data on the percentage of female workers who are in women's jobs and the percentage of workers in those jobs who are female, together with data on their average hourly wage. It shows that over half of all women (57.4 percent) worked in female-dominated occupations as commonly defined.[1] This appendix is distilled in Table 5–1. The first column in Table 5–1 shows the distribution of the female labor force across broad occupational categories in 1980. The second column shows the occupational distribution of women in female-dominated jobs. And the third column shows the occupational distribution of women who are in female-dominated jobs that pay less than the average female wage ($5.22 per hour).

Comparing columns 1 and 2, we note that none of the women in the managerial group and only one-third of the women in the blue-collar categories are in female-dominated Census occupations. Ninety-five percent of all women in female-dominated occupations are employed in the remaining occupational groups—professional and technical, sales, clerical, and service. In all but the professional and technical category there is a strong association between female-dominated occupations and below-average female wages. Thus, while almost 17 percent of women in female-dominated occupations are professional and technical workers, less than 3 percent of all women in low-wage female-dominated occupations are in this category. In contrast,

Table 5–1. The Distribution of Women, Women in Female-Dominated Jobs, and Women in Low-Wage Female-Dominated Jobs across Broad Occupational Groups in 1980.

Occupational Group	(1) Percentage of All Women Workers	(2) Percentage of All Women in Female Occupations	(3) Percentage of All Women in Low-Wage Female Occupations
Managerial	7.2%	0.0%	0.0%
Professional and technical	16.6	16.5	2.8
Sales	11.3	13.4	15.7
Clerical	30.6	43.0	50.0
Service	18.1	22.0	25.6
Blue collar	15.8	5.1	5.9
Total	99.5%[a]	100.0%	100.0%

a. 0.5 percent reported no occupation.
Note: Low wage is defined as less than the mean wage for all women in 1980 ($5.22 per hour).
Source: Appendix 5–A and the sources cited there.

the sales, clerical, and service occupations account for 78 percent of all women in female-dominated jobs and 91 percent of all women in low-wage female-dominated jobs.[2]

Clearly, then, comparable worth is likely to be a white- (and pink-) collar issue. But the mere fact that potential beneficiaries of comparable worth are concentrated in white-collar jobs does not imply that it would benefit women who are already relatively well off. Sales, clerical, and service occupations contain many low-wage jobs, and, as we have just seen, 91 percent of all women in low-wage female-dominated jobs are in these three occupational categories. Thus, while the public emphasis of comparable worth has often been to compare nurses or librarians (two relatively high-wage female-dominated jobs) with tree trimmers or plumbers, many of the potential beneficiaries of comparable worth are in fact women with below-average wages. How comparable worth would be likely to affect different groups is the question we turn to now.

MODELS AND DEFINITIONS

As we have repeatedly pointed out, estimates of the impact of comparable worth depend on how it is defined and on the models employed to estimate its effect. We emphasize that the model on which these comparable worth wage adjustments are based employs very different procedures than those described in Chapter 2 or in the advocate's model in Chapter 4. Most importantly, our approach does not simply "give" workers in female-dominated jobs the wage equation estimated for some other reference group.

Our approach is, instead, to set the effect of percent female to zero, removing just that portion of the wage that is affected by the femaleness of the occupation. This model also allows different corrections for men and women in the same occupation because men and women may differ in their levels on variables (such as experience) that interact with percent female in our model.

In the preceding chapter (Table 4–5) we presented lower- and upper-bound comparable worth wage adjustments for women. Because the lower-bound effects are generally quite small and because (as argued in Chapter 4) we believe that the upper-bound estimates are less affected by the type of sex discrimination we wish to correct for, we confine ourselves to the upper-bound estimates in the present chapter.[3]

Finally, we note that all of the calculations below are partial, not general, equilibrium estimates. Their possible effects on employment, inflation, and other relative prices are ignored. They are best seen, therefore, as short-run effects and are likely to overstate the impact on real annual earnings if the indicated wage adjustment changes output or prices or induces the substitution of capital or cheaper labor for the workers whose wages are raised by comparable worth.

THE IMPACT OF COMPARABLE WORTH

In Chapter 4 we presented an upper-bound estimate that comparable worth, if applied to all jobs, would raise the average wage for all workers by around 6 percent (3 percent for men, 14 percent for women), and if applied only to women's jobs would raise the wage of workers in these jobs by around 14 percent (5 percent for men and 16 percent for women). We now turn to its impact on occupations, occupational classes, and sectors of the labor force. The Census data discussed above suggest that comparable worth would be most likely to benefit white-collar relative to blue-collar jobs. In this sense it might indeed devalue manual labor, as critics have charged. But Census figures also suggest that many of the white-collar jobs most likely to gain from comparable worth pay below-average earnings. This section presents estimates of the impact that our comparable worth adjustment would have on these and various other groups of workers.

THE IMPACT OF COMPARABLE WORTH ON SELECTED GROUPS

We have employed the version of the economist's model described above to estimate the impact that comparable worth applied to all jobs would have on specific occupations and various occupational groups. The effect on some representative occupations is shown in Table 5–2. Here we see that the wage adjustments are substantial (on the order of 15 to 30 percent) for nurses and teachers. They are between 12 for 14 percent for bookkeepers, secretaries, and hospital attendants and nearly 20 percent for assemblers. In contrast, increases in male-dominated jobs are modest (5 percent for welders) to negligible (less than 1 percent for foremen and auto mechanics). The largest increases for women go to nurses, primary and secondary school teachers, and assemblers (despite the fact that the latter two occupations are not especially highly feminized). These estimates of the effect of comparable worth on selected occupations thus tend to support the conclusion that the biggest benefits accrue to professional workers.[4]

We turn now to the impact of comparable worth on broad occupational groups and on public- (versus private-) sector workers. Table 5–3 presents the average comparable worth wage adjustment for workers in female-dominated occupations. These are higher for women than for men primarily because, even among workers in female-dominated occupations, women are in occupations with a higher percentage of female workers than are men. Female-dominated occupations in the public sector receive

Table 5–2. Comparable Worth Wage Adjustments for Workers in Selected Occupations.

Group/Sex	Current Wage	Change $	Change %
Nurses (95.2%)	$7.09	$1.34	18.8%
Men	——	——	——
Women	6.93	1.38	19.9
Elementary school teachers (81.8%)	7.26	2.19	30.1
Men	8.67	2.27	26.2
Women	6.94	2.17	31.2
Secondary school teachers (45.7%)	7.54	1.09	14.5
Men	8.06	1.06	13.2
Women	6.92	1.12	16.2
Bookkeepers (92.4%)	5.29	.59	11.2
Men	——	——	——
Women	5.12	.60	11.8
Secretaries (98.7%)	5.12	.72	14.0
Men	——	——	——
Women	5.07	.73	14.4
Foremen (9.5%)	9.11	.07	0.8
Men	9.47	.07	0.8
Women	——	——	——
Assemblers (56.4%)	6.50	1.22	18.7
Men	7.30	1.13	15.5
Women	5.88	1.29	21.9
Welders (13.7%)	6.46	.39	5.1
Men	7.92	.38	4.8
Women	——	——	——
Auto mechanics (2.3%)	7.18	.02	0.3
Men	7.27	.02	0.3
Women	——	——	——

Table 5–2 *continued*

Group/Sex	Current Wage	Change $	Change %
Hospital attendants (87.5%)	4.15	.56	13.5
Men	—	—	—
Women	3.99	.39	9.7

Notes: Numbers in parentheses are percent female in the occupation. Percentage changes are calculated from unrounded dollar figures. Estimates based on fewer than ten observations are not reported.

Source: Computed using equations (4.2) and (4.4) and levels on independent variables for individual workers and broken down by occupation.

a 17 percent increase versus 12 percent in the private sector. Professional and technical workers in female-dominated occupations get a 19 percent increase, clerical workers an 11 percent increase, sales and service workers a 4 percent increase, and blue-collar workers a whopping 37 percent increase.

These data do not tell us the overall impact of comparable worth on all workers in these various groups, however, because that depends on what portion of workers in each group qualify for an adjustment (that is, what portion are in occupations that are 70 percent or more female). For this information we turn to Table 5–4, where we see the effect on *all* workers in each category of a comparable worth wage adjustment for female-dominated occupations versus one for all occupations in the category. The first of these adjustments amounts to a weighted average of the adjustments given in Table 5–3 for workers in female-dominated occupations and zero adjustments for workers who are not. We present these estimates because they conform most closely to the conventional approach of restricting comparable worth wage adjustments to female-dominated occupations. We present the second estimates because (for reasons discussed in Chapter 4) we believe that a 70 percent cutoff is arbitrary and problematical.

We see in Table 5–4 that if only female-dominated occupations receive a wage adjustment, wage changes for men would be negligible in all occupational groups and sectors. This is because only 8 percent of the men in our sample are in female-dominated occupations, compared to 66 percent of the women.

Table 5–3. The Average Effect of a comparable Worth Wage Adjustment for Workers in Female-Dominated Occupations.

	Current Wage	Change $	Change %
All workers	$5.56	$.75	13.6%
Men	7.80	.38	4.9
Women	5.21	.81	15.6
Public sector	5.84	.99	17.0
Men	8.30	.95	11.4
Women	5.42	1.00	18.4
Private sector	5.44	.66	12.2
Men	7.58	.13	1.7
Women	5.13	.74	14.4
Professional and technical	7.03	1.37	19.4
Men	8.49	1.39	16.3
Women (23.0%/21.2%)	6.78	1.36	20.1
Clerical	5.39	.60	11.2
Men	8.02	− .01	− 0.1
Women (40.8%/57.1%)	4.98	.70	14.1
Retail sales and service	4.75	.19	4.0
Men	6.43	.40	6.3
Women (14.4%/15.2%)	4.48	.16	3.5
Craft, operators, and laborers	3.77	1.40	37.1
Men	—	—	—
Women (18.4%/6.2%)	3.75	1.47	39.1

Notes: Percentage changes are calculated from unrounded dollar figures. Estimates based on fewer than ten observations are not reported.

The numbers in parentheses show the percentages of all women in the sample (first number) and all women in female-dominated occupations (second number) who are in the indicated occupational group. For example, 40.8 percent of all women and 57.1 percent of all women in female-dominated jobs were in clerical occupations. They do not add to 100 because some occupations were excluded from these categories.

Source: Computed using equations (4.2) and (4.4) and levels on independent variables for individual workers and broken down by sector and occupational group.

Table 5–4. The Average Effect for All Workers of a Comparable Worth Wage Adjustment for Female-Dominated Occupations versus an Adjustment for All Occupations.

	Wage	Female-Dominated Occupations		All Occupations	
		Change		Change	
		$	%	$	%
All Workers (43.7%)	$7.04	.25	3.6	.44	6.2
Men	8.36	.03	0.4	.20	2.5
Women	5.33	.53	10.0	.73	13.8
Public sector (50.5%)	6.97	.41	5.9	.67	9.7
Men	8.14	.12	1.4	.40	4.9
Women	5.82	.70	12.1	.94	16.2
Private sector (41.7%)	7.06	.20	2.9	.37	5.2
Men	8.41	.01	0.1	.16	1.9
Women	5.16	.48	9.2	.66	12.8
Professional and technical (44.6%)	8.57	.43	5.0	.70	8.2
Men	9.92	.11	1.2	.35	3.6
Women	6.90	.82	11.9	1.13	16.4
Clerical (78.5%)	5.64	.50	9.0	.56	10.0
Men	7.85	−.01	−0.1	.17	2.1
Women	5.03	.64	12.8	.67	13.4
Retail sales and service (58.2%)	5.41	.09	1.7	.13	2.3
Men	7.00	.06	0.9	.03	0.4
Women	4.26	.11	2.6	.20	4.6
Crafts, operatives, and labor (20.9%)	7.12	.07	1.0	.35	4.9
Men	7.77	.00	0.0	.21	2.7
Women	4.66	.33	7.0	.88	19.0

Note: Numbers in parentheses are percent female in the sector or occupational group.
Source: Computed from equations (4.2) and (4.4) and levels of independent variables for individual workers and broken down by sector and occupational group.

The overall increase for women would be 10 percent, with women in the public sector getting a 12 percent increase and those in the private sector a 9 percent increase. Professional and technical women's wages rise by an average of 12 percent, and female clerical wages rise by nearly 13 percent. The increase for female sales and service workers is less than 3 percent, and for blue-collar women workers is 7 percent.

The pattern of these wage increases is an artifact of the arbitrary 70 percent female cutoff, which weights benefits to occupational groups in proportion to the presence of female-dominated occupations in them. The most striking example of this is in the blue-collar category. Here, a 39 percent increase for women in female-dominated blue-collar occupations raises the average earnings of all blue-collar women by only 7 percent (precisely because there are so few female-dominated blue-collar occupations). Thus, we see that comparable worth wage adjustments restricted to workers in occupations that are at least 70 percent female would indeed benefit white-collar women to a much greater extent than blue-collar women.

If instead we adjust wages in all occupations (with the largest adjustments tending to go to the most highly feminized occupations) we get the pattern of wage adjustments shown in the right-hand side of Table 5–4. This would, of course, yield larger increases for all groups. Men's wages would increase by an average of 2.5 percent (rather than only 0.4 percent), while women's would increase by 13.8 percent (rather than 10.0 percent). Wage increases are 16 percent for female professional and technical workers, 13 percent for female clerical workers, and 19 percent for female blue-collar workers. Female retail sales and service workers (the lowest paid of any of the occupational groups) would get only a 4.6 percent increase.

Thus, under an approach in which all jobs receive a comparable worth wage adjustment, average wage increases are small for men in all occupational categories and range from around 15 percent for white-collar women to 19 percent for blue-collar women down to less than 5 percent for female retail sales and service workers. In terms of the distribution of wage increase among occupational groups, the biggest impact of such an across-the-board application of comparable worth (as opposed to

Table 5–5. The Impact of Comparable Worth on Female/Male Wage Ratios.

Group	Current Ratio	Ratio If Only Female Occupations' Wage Adjusted	Ratio If All Occupations' Wage Adjusted
Female/Male whites	.619	.678	.686
Female/Male blacks	.753	.826	.836
Female/Male all	.638	.699	.708

Source: Table 5–4.

one that is restricted to jobs that are at least 70 percent female) is that it produces much larger average increases for female blue-collar workers.

In Table 5–5 we return to the central question of the effect of comparable worth on the relative earnings of men and women. As this table shows, our (upper-bound) comparable worth wage adjustments would raise the overall female/male wage ratio for our sample from 64 percent to 70 or 71 percent—depending on whether adjustments were made only for female-dominated jobs or for all jobs. Thus, our comparable worth wage adjustment would reduce the 36 percentage point wage gap by 6 or 7 percentage points—a roughly 15 to 20 percent reduction in the male/female wage gap. As the other ratios in Table 5–5 indicate, we get similar increases when the ratio is broken down by race. And in all cases the increase is about one percentage point bigger if all occupations are adjusted than if only those that are at least 70 percent female are adjusted.

COMPARABLE WORTH AND THE DISTRIBUTION OF LABOR EARNINGS

Apparently some poorly paid female blue-collar workers would benefit more than average from comparable worth, but so would some relatively highly paid professionals. These break-downs of the impact of comparable worth on different occupational groups therefore do not give us a definitive answer concerning the impact of comparable worth on the overall wage distribution. In this section we investigate the overall distributional impact of our comparable worth adjustments and their effect on the relative earnings of blacks and whites.

IMPACT ON THE OVERALL DISTRIBUTION OF WAGES

Table 5–6 presents data on the distribution of labor earnings by quintile among individuals in our sample of workers together with the average wage for each group. The second column in Table 5–6 shows the quintile shares of current wages, before any adjustment. The third and fourth columns show the wage shares of each quintile after our two comparable worth wage adjustments. As can be seen in this table, the share of the top quintile falls, the share of the second and third quintiles remains roughly the same, and the share of the bottom two quintiles increases from either version of a comparable worth wage adjustment. The Gini coefficient for the wage distribution declines by 4.9 percent if only female-dominated occupations receive a wage adjustment versus 7.4 percent if all occupations do. The more comprehensive approach (adjusting wages for all occupations) thus has a more equalizing effect than if wages were adjusted only in female-dominated occupations. But either approach produces a substantial equalizing effect.[5]

Given that women are paid so much less than men on the average, it is not surprising that a comparable worth wage adjustment that raises women's wages substantially more than men's produces an equalizing effect on the overall wage distribution. What is less clear, however, is the effect of these wage adjustments on the distribution of women's wages. It is, of course, quite possible for a given wage adjustment to reduce the inequality of earnings overall even while it increases inequality among women. Our analysis of wage changes in various occupational classes was ambiguous on this question, but the relatively large increases for professional workers and negligible increases for retail sales and service workers suggested that comparable worth as we have defined it might increase earnings inequality among women even while it reduced inequality between men and women.

The wage distributions in Table 5–7 address this issue, and they indicate that comparable worth would not increase earnings

Table 5–6. Impact of Alternative Comparable Worth Wage Adjustments on the Distribution of Labor Earnings.

Quintile	Mean Wage	Percentage of All Wages	After Comparable Worth Adjustment for:	
			Female-Dominated Occupations	All Occupations
Top	$12.60	35.8%	35.0%	34.5%
Second	8.38	23.8	23.6	23.6
Middle	6.33	18.0	18.2	18.3
Fourth	4.77	13.6	14.1	14.2
Bottom	3.09	8.8	9.2	9.4
Gini Ratio		.2574	.2448	.2384
Change in Gini Ratio		—	-4.9%	-7.4%

Source: Computed using equations (4.2) and (4.4) and levels on independent variables for individual workers.

inequality among women. If only women in female-dominated occupations receive wage adjustments, the share of the top quintile falls and the share of the third and fourth rises. Although the share of the bottom quintile actually falls slightly (by .1 percentage point), the overall effect is towards greater equality, as the 3.1 percent decline in the Gini coefficient shows. On the other hand, if all occupations are eligible for a wage adjustment (right-hand column, Table 5–7), the shares of the top two quintiles fall and the shares of the bottom two rise. These changes produce a 6.5 percent decrease in the Gini coefficient. Thus, we see that comparable worth, as we have defined it, would have almost as great an equalizing effect on women's wages alone as it would on all (men's and women's) wages.

IMPACT ON THE BLACK/WHITE WAGE RATIO

The question of the relative effect on the wages of blacks and whites of our comparable worth adjustments is addressed in Tables 5–8 and 5–9. Table 5–8 shows that for both men and women, our comparable worth wage adjustments raise black and white workers' average wages by just about the same dollar amount, making the percentage increase larger for blacks. Table 5–9 shows the effect of this on the black/white wage ratio, which (comparing the first and last columns) increases by 1 percentage point for men, 1.5 percentage points for women, and 2 percentage points for all blacks relative to all whites. As the second row from the bottom shows, this gain in the overall black/white ratio is due primarily to a 7 percentage point gain (from .54 to .61) in the ratio of black women's to white women's wages. Black men would gain only slightly compared to white men and would lose in comparison to white women. Thus, while comparable worth does not specifically aim to reduce racial inequality, our model would in fact achieve a modest 1 to 2 percentage point (4 to 8 percent) reduction in the black/white earnings gap.

CONCLUSION

Is comparable worth a middle-class, white women's issue? Our answer to this question is a qualified no. Comparable worth is, of course, necessarily a women's issue. This is inherent in its

Table 5–7. Impact of Comparable Worth on the Distribution of Labor Earnings among Women Workers.

Quintile	Mean Wage	Percentage of All Wages	After Comparable Worth Adjustment for: Female-Dominated Occupations	All Occupations
Top	$9.23	34.6%	33.8%	33.4%
Second	6.17	23.2	23.3	23.1
Middle	4.84	18.2	18.6	18.5
Fourth	3.80	14.3	14.7	14.9
Bottom	2.61	9.8	9.7	10.1
Gini Ratio		.2342	.2270	.2191
Change in Gini Ratio		—	−3.1%	−6.5%

Source: Computed using equations (4.2) and (4.4) and levels on independent variables for individual workers.

Table 5–8. The Impact of Comparable Worth on Black and White Wages.

Group/Sex	Current Wage	Female-Dominated Occupations		All Occupations	
		Change		Change	
Blacks (45.7%)	$5.66	$.26	4.6%	$.48	8.6%
Men	6.45	.03	0.4	.24	3.7
Women	4.85	.50	10.2	.74	15.2
Whites (43.1%)	7.51	.25	3.3	.42	5.6
Men	8.93	.03	0.3	.19	2.2
Women	5.52	.55	10.0	.73	13.3

Note: Numbers in parentheses are percentage of females in the sector or occupational group.

Source: Computed from equations (4.2) and (4.4) and levels on independent variables for individual workers.

aim of increasing wages in jobs primarily performed by women. Men in these jobs benefit too, but there are relatively few of them. As a result, many more women than men will benefit, and comparable worth, as we have defined it, will reduce the male/female wage gap by 15 to 20 percent.

Comparable worth clearly benefits white-collar (professional, technical, and clerical) women, regardless of whether all occupations or only female-dominated ones receive an adjustment. On the other hand, women in female-dominated service jobs receive

Table 5–9. The Impact of Comparable Worth on Black/White Wage Ratios.

Group	Current Ratio	Ratio if Only Female Occ. Wage Adjusted	Ratio if All Occs. Wage Adjusted
Black/white men	.722	.722	.733
Black/white women	.878	.881	.893
Black women/white men	.543	.597	.612
Black/white all	.754	.763	.775

Source: Table 5–8.

minimal wage increases. Blue-collar women in female-dominated jobs get the largest increases of all. But since relatively few blue-collar occupations are female dominated, the overall gain for blue-collar women is small if adjustments are restricted to occupations that are 70 percent or more female. On the other hand, if all occupations get wage adjustments, blue-collar women receive the largest average wage increase of any group. We conclude that comparable worth as we have defined it, applied to all occupations rather than restricted to those above some arbitrary percentage female cutoff, would benefit blue-collar women as much or more than white-collar women. The occupational group that appears to be excluded from the benefits of comparable worth is the one out of seven women (in our sample) in retail sales and service jobs.

On the question of race we decisively reject the charge that comparable worth favors whites. Dollar gains from comparable worth are very nearly the same for blacks and whites, and percentage gains are larger for blacks (since their initial wages are lower). A small reduction in the black/white earnings gap is therefore a by-product of our comparable worth wage adjustments.

Finally, we find that comparable worth wage increases would reduce wage inequality among all workers. This is to be expected, since women are paid so much less than men, and they receive most of the increases. But comparable worth would reduce wage inequality *among women* too. We find that, whether comparable worth is applied narrowly (to female-dominated occupations only) or broadly (to all occupations) the share of the top quintile of women falls, but in the narrow application so does the share of the bottom quintile. This is a result of the negligible gains for low-wage sales and service workers noted above. These are the only shreds of evidence that comparable worth would have any inequalitarian consequences. However, by the single most comprehensive measure of inequality—the Gini coefficient—either approach reduces the degree of inequality in women's wages.

In sum, our investigation of the distributional impact of comparable worth does not support its opponents' charges that it benefits white, middle-class women at the expense of other groups.

APPENDIX 5–A
WOMEN'S EMPLOYMENT AND EARNINGS IN OCCUPATIONS THAT ARE MORE THAN 70 PERCENT FEMALE: 1980

Occupation	Number of Women	Percentage of All Women Workers	Percent Female	Mean Female Wage
Female labor force	44,304,473	100	42.6	$5.22
In female jobs	25,443,399	57.42		
Professional	3,475,206	7.85	49.1	—
Registered Nurse	1,232,544	2.78	95.6	6.98
Dietitian	60,483	.14	89.9	5.90
Occupational therapist	16,257	.04	91.6	6.55
Physical therapist	31,841	.07	73.9	7.00
Speech therapist	36,811	.08	89.1	6.86
Health specialty teacher	16,955	.04	86.7	7.75
Kindergarten teacher	176,744	.40	96.4	3.98
Elementary school teacher	1,749,547	3.95	75.4	6.27
Librarian	154,600	.35	82.5	6.70
Technical	730,491	1.65	64.4	—
Clinical laboratory technician	181,807	.41	74.5	6.15
Dental hygienist	45,484	.10	98.5	6.57
Health record technician	13,833	.03	91.3	5.76
Radiologic technician	68,955	.16	71.6	5.81
Practical nurse	420,412	.95	96.5	4.87
Sales occupations	3,417,840	7.71	48.7	—
Retail sales[a]	3,417,840	7.71	78.7	4.04

APPENDIX 5–A *continued*

Occupation	Number of Women	Percentage of All Women Workers	Percent Female	Mean Female Wage
Clerical	10,920,018	24.66	77.1	—
Secretary	3,949,973	8.92	98.3	5.14
Stenographer	79,633	.18	90.9	5.23
Typist	716,449	1.62	96.8	4.64
Information clerk[a]	709,901	1.60	95.8	4.40
Records processing except financial[a]	566,985	1.28	82.0	4.72
Records processing financial[a]	2,005,818	4.53	89.1	4.99
Common equipment operator[a]	286,894	.65	90.8	4.97
Misc. administrative supervisor[a]	2,604,365	5.88	85.3	4.69
Service	5,602,981	12.65	58.9	—
Private household	597,451	1.35	96.3	
Food preparation*	1,581,189	3.57	86.7	3.15
Health service*	1,611,254	3.64	88.1	4.03
Maids and houseman	510,277	1.15	75.8	3.43
Hairdresser	490,785	1.11	87.8	4.12
Public transportation attendant	54,641	.12	78.1	6.72
Welfare service aide	53,730	.12	88.4	3.80
Child care worker	570,794	1.29	93.2	2.67
Personal service not elsewhere classified	132,860	.30	72.5	3.60
Craft	182,436	.41	7.8	—
Dressmaker	97,154	.22	93.5	3.58

APPENDIX 5–A *continued*

Occupation	Number of Women	Percentage of All Women Workers	Percent Female	Mean Female Wage
Electrical equipment assembler	85,282	.19	75.8	4.75
Operatives and laborers	1,107,612	2.50	27.4	—
Textile winding and twisting machine operator	83,775	.19	75.2	4.07
Textile sew machine operator	860,848	1.94	94.1	3.62
Shoe machine operator	56,530	.13	73.9	3.65
Press machine operator	80,571	.18	75.1	3.44
Solderer and brazer	26,457	.06	78.0	4.38

Source: U.S. Bureau of the Census (1984a, 1984b).
a. Several detailed occupations are grouped in these categories

NOTES

1. We note that almost 66 percent of the women in our NLS sample are in women's jobs, as opposed to just 57 percent of the Census women. Most of this disparity results from the exclusion of managerial occupations (none of which are female dominated) from our sample. However, the mean wages of women in our sample were $5.33, quite close to the mean of $5.22 for the Census women.
2. Of course, low wage does not *necessarily* mean underpaid. Nevertheless, our approach to adjusting wages for the devaluation of women's jobs is very likely to give the biggest adjustments to the most highly female-dominated occupations.
3. Recall that the upper-bound estimates are based on equation (4.4), which uses regression coefficients estimated from the male sample and levels of percent female and the other independent variables based on the female sample.
4. Our lower-bound estimates of the effect of percent female on women's wages (and the resulting comparable worth wage adjustment) give sharply different results for some of these occupations. In particular, lower-bound adjustments (using regression coefficients estimated from the female sample instead of the male sample) *reduce* female nurses and elementary school teachers wages by $.58

and $.50, respectively. What this means is that in a labor market where women face discrimination everywhere, the opportunity cost of being in those particular occupations is much lower for women than it is for men. Our upper-bound estimate is taken here as a preferable measure of the undervaluation of these jobs, though it is possibly an overestimate and, given discrimination, certainly overstates the opportunity cost to women of taking these jobs.

5. To put these changes in perspective we note that between 1965 and 1979 the share of money income of the bottom quintile of all families varied between 5.2 and 5.6 percent. In this context increases of 0.4 and 0.6 percentage points are substantial. On the other hand, they are not unprecedented either. As a case in point the 1981–82 recession and welfare cuts reduced the money income share of the bottom fifth of all families by 0.5 percentage points between 1979 and 1981 (Buchele 1984).

BIBLIOGRAPHY

Buchele, Robert. 1984. "Reaganomics and the Fairness Issue." *Challenge* 24 (Sept./Oct.):25–31.

Comparable Worth Project Newsletter 1982–1985. Oakland, Calif.

Katz, Lee Michael. 1985. "Talking Tough (Interview with Linda Chavez." *Washington Woman* 2 (March):17 + .

New York Times. 1982–1985.

U.S. Bureau of the Census. 1984a. 1980 Census of Population. *Detailed Occupation of the Experienced Civilian Labor Force by Sex for the United States and Regions: 1970 and 1980.* Washington, D.C.: GPO.

_____. 1984b. 1980 Census of Population. *Earnings by Occupation and Education.* Washington, D.C.: GPO.

Washington Post. 1982–1985.

CHAPTER 6

The Impact of Comparable
Worth on Employment

There would be massive job dislocations [from comparable worth].
-JUNE O'NEILL of the Urban Institute

(Wall Street Journal, July 8, 1985:16).

There's no evidence that jobs will be lost.
-CLAUDIA WAYNE of the National Committee on Pay Equity

(Wall Street Journal, July 8, 1985:16.)

INTRODUCTION

However one may define or implement comparable worth, it would raise relative earnings in women's jobs. In Chapter 4, we estimated this increase would average about 14 percent, although the exact amount is sensitive to the way comparable worth is defined and varies substantially from job to job. In this chapter we address the obvious question: Wouldn't such a policy sharply reduce employment in female-dominated occupations? As usual, we begin by looking at what economic theory has to say on this matter. We then review the U.S. experience with minimum wages and the recent Australian experiment with comparable worth. Finally, we estimate the employment effect both within and between occupations that would result from the comparable worth wage adjustments that we calculated in Chapter 5. We tentatively conclude that if comparable worth were to raise women's earnings by 10 to 15 percent relative to men's within the broad occupational groups defined in Chapter 5, total employment in them would fall roughly 1 to 4 percent, and women's employment in them would fall an additional 1 to 2 percent. Focusing specifically on female-dominated jobs, we find that an increase in the relative earnings of all female jobs of about 13 percent would reduce their employment by around 3 percent.

THE EMPLOYMENT EFFECTS OF LEGISLATED WAGE INCREASES IN THEORY

The implementation of comparable worth would affect employment in much the same way that the minimum wage does. If all jobs were subject to comparable worth adjustments, the result would be to raise relative earnings in the most female-dominated occupations. And if only female jobs were affected, there would be a "covered sector" of the economy within which wages would rise by varying amounts and an "uncovered" sector that would be unaffected. This is almost exactly the way the minimum wage has operated in the United States. Accordingly, we look to both the theoretical analyses of the minimum wage and the empirical assessments of its impact for guidance in evaluating the likely employment effects of comparable worth.

Almost everyone who has ever taken an introductory economics course remembers—if only dimly—the conclusion that a minimum wage causes unemployment. Usually the analysis involves a simple supply and demand diagram. First, the instructor reminds the class that the wage for a job is set by the interaction of labor supply and demand. If the labor market is assumed to be competitive, and the market clearing wage for the job is (say) $2.50 per hour, then a legislated minimum of $3.00 per hour would reduce the quantity of labor demanded and thus employment in this job. The instructor might then go on to note that not all jobs are covered by minimum wage legislation and that those who lose jobs in the covered sector may seek employment in the uncovered sector, thereby driving down wages there.

This simple supply and demand model of minimum wages with incomplete coverage provides, with some customizing, a tolerable approximation of the employment effects of comparable worth. Thus, the straightforward and gloomy prediction would be that comparable worth will reduce employment in women's jobs and either reduce wages elsewhere or reduce total employment, or both. However, this is the sort of analysis that got economics labeled the dismal science, and there are several reasons why these predicted effects might not come about.

First, the model assumes that the relevant markets are competitive, and as even the opponents of comparable worth agree, at least some of the labor markets in which women work are dominated by employer cartels. As we noted in Chapter 3, there is evidence of employer collusion in some local labor markets for nurses and clerical workers. This is an example of monopsony, and if employers were forced by comparable worth to pay a higher wage in such a situation, employment might even *rise* because employers would no longer face a situation in which they could suppress wages by restricting hiring.

Another reason that minimum wages or comparable worth may not reduce the number of people employed in women's job is because employers could respond by cutting the hours of existing employees rather than reducing the number of workers. Most discussions of the minimum wage simply fudge this question and assume that reductions in the quantity of labor demanded will take the form of reductions in the number of workers rather than reductions in hours per worker (Cherry 1982). Yet clearly this need not happen. For example, secretaries in a firm that implemented comparable worth, thereby raising wages by (say) 10 percent, might find their numbers unchanged but their work week shortened from (say) 35 hours to 32 hours, or by about 9 percent. In this case comparable worth would not cause unemployment, and it would raise the earnings of all workers in the covered job without reducing earnings elsewhere.

Finally, comparable worth might not cause unemployment if the wage increase itself caused a sufficiently large increase in labor productivity so that labor costs (wage costs per dollar of output), and hence employment, remained unaffected. This could happen if the wage increase were to motivate workers to work harder, or if it stimulated employers to reorganize production in ways that enhanced worker productivity. While such events sound like wishful thinking, there are a number of documented cases in which raising wages has stimulated worker productivity.[1] And there is much evidence that large, bureaucratic organizations operate with considerable economic slack. The business press regularly reports instances of firms that have responded to competitive pressures by cutting costs drastically. Thus, it is at least possible that a policy that raised wages could also enhance productivity enough to offset any effects on costs.[2]

In short, the traditional microeconomic prediction that minimum wages or comparable worth would reduce employment in the covered sector need not always hold, either in theory or in fact. But whether a given comparable worth wage increase would in fact reduce employment (and if so, by how much) is ultimately an empirical, not a theoretical, matter. In the remainder of this chapter we review some of the evidence on this issue and then present our own estimates of the employment effects of comparable worth.

THE EVIDENCE ON EMPLOYMENT EFFECTS

No subject in economics has been more thoroughly investigated than the employment effects of wage legislation. Almost all economists believe that legal efforts to raise wages result in some unemployment, while supporters of such laws tend to downplay any adverse consequences. Here we review some of the evidence on this issue from U.S. history and Australia's recent experience with comparable worth.

MINIMUM WAGE LAWS

As Chapter 1 described, minimum wage laws for women date back to the turn of this century. Supporters of this early legislation never developed a clear position on whether it would restrict women's employment. Some of them clearly saw it not only as a way to protect women but also as a means of protecting men from female competition, thus clearly acknowledging its negative impact on female employment. This argument was employed as late as the 1930s to justify the equal pay clauses in the National Recovery Act Codes and in the 1940s to support the first federal equal pay bills.

Early opponents of protective legislation such as Rhetta Childe Dorr, agreed that such laws would limit the ability of women to compete with men, but this was hardly to be desired, she thought. Dorr, a supporter of the first Equal Rights Amendment, argued in the 1925 in the pages of *Good Housekeeping* when we limit women's opportunities to work, we simply create more poverty (Dorr 1925:160).

In response to these charges, some supporters of protective legislation denied that it would reduce women's employment, and a few even tried to have their cake and eat it too, arguing that such laws would *improve* women's employent prospects. Responding to Dorr in the same issue of *Good Housekeeping,* Mary Anderson of the Women's Bureau argued that

it is in the states that have good laws for women workers that there exist . . . the most important examples of women's advance into new fields of employment (Anderson 1925:167).

This happy conclusion appears to be based more on wish than on fact, however. It is true that some early state laws probably had little impact, but this was because they were not enforced or were "enforced" only in instances where wages were already above the required minimum. Several careful case studies of these early laws suggest that they probably did cause reductions in female employment in the jobs they covered (Peterson 1959).

Research on the impact of federal minimum wages since World War II largely confirms these findings. We are fortunate that several recent studies have provided excellent surveys of much of the minimum wage literature, and we rely heavily on these works. Most of the minimum wage studies focus on its impact on teenage employment (since these least experienced and presumably least productive workers are the group most affected by the minimum wage). All the studies use multiple regression techniques with varying functional forms and controls and cover different time periods from the mid-1950s on. With a few exceptions, the general consensus from the analyses that employ time series data is that a 10 percent rise in the minimum wage would reduce teenage employment by 1 to 3 percent (Brown, Gilroy, and Kohen 1982).

Cross-section data indicate somewhat larger impacts, while studies of older adults (age 20 to 24) suggest smaller effects. In all, however, the results are reasonably clear: Minimum wage increases do generate a small net reduction in employment for affected groups. Note, however, that the impact on some groups of workers and jobs may be larger than these findings suggest. The 1 to 3 percent estimates pertain to the net impact on all teenagers and all jobs. The least-skilled teenagers (or those in the least-skilled jobs) will be the most likely to lose their jobs as a result of the minimum wage. And if employment in the uncovered sector rises and partly offsets job losses in the covered sector, then obviously the employment response of the covered sector to minimum wages is greater than the net effect on the two sectors combined.

We conclude this review of minimum wage laws with a Scotch verdict. The weight of the evidence suggests small but significant net employment declines from such wage policies. We emphasize that one need not conclude that such policies are undesirable, for the employment effects are only one result of such wage increases. However, those who argue that employment declines would *not* flow from the implementation of comparable worth wage increases surely bear the burden of proof to support such a conclusion. As we show in the next section, the Australian experience with comparable worth suggests such an argument would be difficult to sustain.

COMPARABLE WORTH DOWN UNDER

In Australia, wages are regulated by state and federal tribunals that set minimum rates of pay for most jobs.[3] In 1969 the federal tribunal introduced a policy of equal pay for equal work within jobs, to be fully implemented by January of 1972. In 1972 a policy of equal pay for jobs of equal value was decreed to be implemented in three steps by June of 1975. As a result of these policies and perhaps other influences as well, the female-to-male wage ratio rose from .607 in 1971 to .766 in 1977—an increase of 26 percent or 3.8 percent per annum over the six-year period.

Gregory and Duncan (1981) estimated the impact of this rise in women's relative earnings on their employment growth and unemployment rates. They estimated an economywide elasticity of substitution between female and male workers of .3, meaning that a 10 percent increase in the female-to-male earnings ratio would result in a 3 percent fall in the ratio of female-to-male employment. Since women's relative earnings were rising by 3.8 percent per year after 1971, this implies that their employment growth was $3.8^{-.3} = 1.5$ percent per year less than it otherwise would have been. Since female employment actually grew by about 3 percent per year, the rise in relative earnings must have reduced employment growth by $1.5/(3.0 + 1.5) = 33$ percent per year.

Female unemployment may also have risen due to the sharp rise in relative female earnings. Gregory and Duncan also estimated a female unemployment equation of the form

$$U^f = .026(W^f/W^m) + controls$$

Since the wage ratio rose about 16 points after 1971, this implies an increase in the unemployment rate of .4 points. Given that unemployment for women averaged about 3 percent during these years, this represents an increase of $.4/(3.0 - .4) = 15$ percent.[4]

MODELS OF EMPLOYMENT AND RELATIVE EARNINGS

We use two different economic models to analyze the potential employment impact of the comparable worth wage adjustments estimated in Chapters 4 and 5. We first analyze male/female relative wages and employment within occupations. We then turn to the effect of occupational wage changes on employment in broad occupational categories. Finally, we estimate the employment effects on female and other jobs of a comparable worth wage adjustment.

WAGES AND EMPLOYMENT WITHIN JOBS

Based on our economist's model we estimated in Chapter 4 above that comparable worth could increase relative female earnings within occupations. If so, it might then affect these occupations' sex composition as employers would presumably substitute relatively cheaper male for female labor. A common approach to estimating how much of this kind of substitution might occur is to hypothesize an economywide constant elasticity of substitution (CES) production function. If employers are cost minimizers, the following equation for relative female employment (E^f/E^m) as a function of relative wages (W^f/W^m) and control variables can be derived from the CES production function:

$$\ln(E^f/E^m) = a + b\ln(W^f/W^m) + \text{controls} \tag{6.1}$$

where the coefficient b is (minus) the estimated elasticity of substitution between male and female labor, and the controls are the usual human capital and industry and regional variables (Freeman and Medoff 1982:222; Ehrenberg and Smith 1984:27).

With two factors of production the constant output elasticities of demand for female labor with respect to women's and men's wages are

$$\begin{aligned}\varepsilon^{ff} &= -b(1-S^f) \\ &= -bS^m \text{ (since } S^m = 1-S^f\text{), and} \\ \varepsilon^{fm} &= bS^m\end{aligned} \tag{6.2}$$

where S^f and S^m are female and male shares in total compensation and b is the elasticity of substitution (Allen 1938:369–74). The impact of wage changes W^f and W^m on women's employment within any given occupation is calculated as the sum of the own wage and other wage effects:

$$\begin{aligned}\%\Delta E^f &= -bS^m(\%\Delta W^f) + bS^m(\%\Delta W^m), \text{ or} \\ \%\Delta E^f &= bS^m(\%\Delta W^m - \%\Delta W^f)\end{aligned} \tag{6.3}$$

Table 6–1 reports estimates of the elasticity of substitution, b, in equation (6.1), using three-digit industry-occupation means of each variable as the unit of observation. While the sign and magnitude of these estimates seem reasonable, they are not signifi-

Table 6–1. Determinants of Male and Female Employment within Occupations.

Variable	(1)	(2)	(3)
W^f/W^m	$-.548$	$-.335$	$-.348$
	(1.25)	(.84)	(.83)
R^2	.03	.14	.17
F	2.16	2.97	2.99
N	97	97	97

Note: Values in parentheses are t-ratios. Equation (1) controls for schooling, experience, and job tenure. Equation (2) controls for race, unionization, and industry, and location. Equation (3) includes all these controls.

cantly different from zero. It is possible that the production function itself is misspecified, since it includes no measure of capital services (Hammermesh and Grant 1979), but a more serious difficulty may be that the small number of observations in each industry-occupation "cell" has resulted in large sampling errors and imprecise estimates.

While one should obviously take these results with a grain of salt, we can still use them to obtain a rough estimate of the likely fall in female employment within occupations that would result from our predicted comparable worth wages adjustments. Table 6–2 presents such calculations for broad occupational groups, using the elasticity of substitution of .348 estimated in Table 6–1 and the wage increases shown in Table 5–4, above. These estimates suggest that female employment *within* jobs would decline by an average of around 1 percent from a typical comparable worth wage adjustment. This result is broadly consistent with the estimates of Ehrenberg and Smith (1984), who employed similar techniques with different data and who found no within-occupational employment effects at all.

INTEROCCUPATIONAL CHANGES IN WAGES AND EMPLOYMENT

Of course, comparable worth would not simply raise women's relative earnings within jobs. It would also increase the earnings of all workers in relatively female jobs compared to workers in other jobs. Hence, we would expect employment effects between jobs as employers react to comparable worth by substituting "male jobs" for "female jobs" in the production process. For example, just as the increasing comparative costs of doctors has induced hospitals to employ nurses to do what was once done by physicians, so a comparable worth adjustment for nurses would be likely to result in their replacement in some tasks by orderlies. But while this argument seems plausible, the relevant question is, as always, how important would such effects be?

To predict potential interoccupational effects of comparable worth it would be desirable to estimate substitution elasticities between narrowly defined occupations such as nurses and doctors. However, this procedure would imply a separate equation for each occupation and require the (simultaneous) estimation of

Table 6–2. Changes in Female Employment within Broad Occupational Groups Due to a Comparable Worth Wage Adjustment.

Occupational Group	Percent Female	Female Wage	Relative Wage Change	Change in Female Employment
Professional and technical	44.6%	$6.90	+12.8%	−0.8%
Clerical	78.5	5.03	+11.3	−0.2
Retail sales and service	58.2	4.26	+ 4.2	−0.1
Crafts, operatives, and laborers	20.9	4.66	+16.3	−1.5

S_m in equation (6.3) is computed as the percent male in an occupational group times that group's share of the total wage bill.
Source: Computed from data in right-hand column of Table 5–4 using equation (6.3) in the text and an elasticity of substitution of .348 from Table 6–1.

some 300 such equations. Data and computational limitations obviously preclude such an ambitious analysis, and in the following we are forced to employ much more aggregative categories that, while more tractable, may mask a good deal of the interoccupational employment changes that comparable worth would engender.

We begin by aggregating all occupations into three categories: (1) professional and technical workers (2) clerical, sales, and service workers, and (3) craft, operative, and laboring workers.[5] If we then assume that employers throughout the economy minimize the costs specified by a translog cost function in which the wage of each of these occupational groups is an argument, the following three share equations can be derived:

$$S_1 = b_1 + a_{11}lnW_1 + a_{12}lnW_2 + a_{13}lnW_3$$
$$S_2 = b_2 + a_{21}lnW_1 + a_{22}lnW_2 + a_{23}lnW_3 \qquad (6.4)$$
$$S_3 = b_3 + a_{31}lnW_1 + a_{32}lnW_2 + a_{33}lnW_3$$

where S_i is the share of occupation group i in the total wage bill, lnW_j is the natural log of occupation j's mean wage, and a_{ij} is the effect of a unit change in lnW_j on occupation group i's share of the wage bill.

Because the shares must add to 100 percent, these equations are not independent: If two are known, the third is determined. For this reason, we drop the third equation and estimate the first two only. These were estimated with the wage variables entered directly and also (because wages are not exogenous for the economy as a whole) using instrumental variables (wages "predicted" from prior regressions of wages on workers' personal and job characteristics, and a set of industry and regional variables). In addition, each equation was estimated with unconstrained coefficients and also subject to the following homogeneity and symmetry constraints: Homogeneity implies that a doubling of all wages leaves relative shares unchanged, and hence that

$$a_{i1} + a_{i2} + a_{i3} = 0, \text{ for all i} \qquad (6.5)$$

Symmetry means that the effect of W_i on S_j equal that of W_j on S_i, or

$$a_{ij} = a_{ji}, \text{ for i j} \qquad (6.6)$$

The results of an iterative three-stage least squares estimation of this model using instrumental variables and restricted coefficients (that is, equations (6.4) to (6.6)) along with the constant output elasticities of demand that these estimates imply, are reported in Table 6–3. We spare the reader a presentation of the equations estimated without instrumental variables or constraints. They are quite similar to the results shown, and none of the conclusions that follow are particularly sensitive to estimation techniques.

These results allow us to calculate predicted employment changes that would result for these occupational groups from a comparable worth wage adjustment. We report two different estimates in Part B of Table 6–3—the change in employment based on the assumption of constant output and the change based on the assumption of a constant wage bill. The first of these estimates simply sums the effects of the given wage changes using the constant output elasticities of demand reported in Part A of the table according to the formula

$$\%\Delta E_i = \Sigma_j \varepsilon_{ij} \%\Delta W_j \qquad (6.7)$$

The second estimate is based on an equation obtained by taking the total derivative of the share of occupation i, assuming the total employment budget or wage bill is held constant:[6]

$$\%\Delta E_i = [(1/S_i)\ \Sigma_j\ a_{ij} \%\Delta W_j] - \%\Delta W_i \qquad (6.8)$$

These two approaches yield what may be thought of as upper- and lower-bound estimates of the interoccupational employment effects of the comparable worth wage adjustments reported in Table 5–4. Employment is, of course, reduced considerably more under the assumption of a constant wage bill than it is under the assumption of constant output—the constant wage bill estimates ranging between −6 percent and −8 percent and the constant output estimates ranging between zero and +3 percent. Probably neither of these extreme assumptions is very likely. If we take the midpoint of each range as our best estimate of the employment effect of our comparable worth wage increases, we get effects ranging from around −4.0 percent for professional and technical jobs to around −1.4 percent for blue-collar jobs.

Table 6–3. Translog Cost Share Equations for Broad Occcupational Groups and Predicted Employment Changes from a Comparable Worth Wage Adjustment for All Occupations.

A. Share Equations and Implied Own Wage and Cross Elasticities[a]

Occupational Group	lnW1	lnW2	lnW3	W1	W2	W3
1. Professional and technical	+.084 (0.83)	−.100 (1.22)	+.017 (0.18)	−.40	+.07	+.62
2. Clerical, sales, and service	−.100 (1.22)	+.265 (2.11)	−.164 (1.73)	+.08	+.13	+.08
3. Craft, operative, and laborer	+.017	−.164	+.148	+.41	+.05	−.17

B. Predicted Employment Changes

Occupational Group	Wage Change	Change in Employment Assuming:	
		Constant Output[b]	Constant Wage Bill
Professional and technical jobs	+8.2%	+0.3%	−8.2%
Clerical, sales, and service jobs	+7.5	+2.0	−6.4
Craft, operative, and laborer jobs	+4.9	+2.9	−5.6

a. Computed from following formulas for the own wage and cross-elasticity of demand for a factor of production (see Berndt and Wood 1975:261 or Freeman and Medoff 1982:222–3):

$$\epsilon_{ii} = (a_{ii} + S_i^2 - S_i)/S_i \qquad \text{and} \qquad \epsilon_{ij} = (a_{ij} - S_i S_j)/S_i$$

b. The alternative estimates of the change in employment due to our comparable worth wage adjustment are calcuted according to equations (6.7) and (6.8) in the text.

Notes: All equations also contain a constant term. The third equation was not estimated but derived from the other two. Values in parentheses are t-ratios. The instrumental variables used to predict wages were job education and training requirements, worker schooling, experience, tenure and race, and the industry and regional controls. Wage changes are from Table 5–4. Clerical, sales, and service is a weighted average of those two groups.

Table 6–4. Translog Cost Shares for Female-Dominated and Other Jobs, and Predicted Employment Changes from a Comparable Worth Wage Adjustment for All Occupations.

A. Share Equations and Implied Own Wage and Cross Elasticities[a]

Occupational Group	lnW1	lnW2	W1	W2
1. Female jobs	+.221 (1.90)	−.221 (1.90)	+.07	+.01
2. Other jobs	−.221	+.221	+.04	+.06

B. Predicted Employment Changes

Occupational Group	Wage Change	Change in Employment Assuming:	
		Constant Output[b]	Constant Wage Bill
1. Female jobs	+13.6%	+1.1%	−6.0%
2. Other jobs	+ 3.6	+0.7	−5.8

a. Computed from following formulas for the own wage and cross-elasticity of demand for a factor of production (see Berndt and Wood 1975:261 or Freeman and Medoff 1982:222–3):

$$\epsilon_{ii} = (a_{ii} + S_i^2 - S_i)/S_i \qquad \text{and} \qquad \epsilon_{ij} = (a_{ij} - S_i S_j)/S_i$$

b. The alternative estimates of the change in employment due to our comparable worth wage adjustment are calcuted according to equations (6.7) and (6.8) in the text.

Notes: All equations also contain a constant term. The second equation was not estimated but derived from the first. Values in parentheses are t-ratios. The instrumental variables used to predict wages were job education and training requirements, worker schooling, experience, tenure and race, and the industry and regional controls. The wage change for female dominated jobs is from Table 5–3. The wage change for other jobs is not reported in Chapter 5.

We have also used a translog specification to estimate changes in employment between female-dominated jobs (defined as usual to contain at least 70 percent women) and other jobs. Again, the equations were estimated both directly and using instrumental variables, and with and without restrictions. Estimates using instruments and restrictions are presented in Part A Table 6–4. While these coefficients appear to be statistically significant, the own-wage elasticities that they imply are positive. This is not terribly plausible and calculations based on such estimates clearly call for a few more grains of salt. Nevertheless we have employed them in equations (6.7) and (6.8) to estimate employment changes for these two categories of jobs. These results are also presented in Part B of Table 6–4. They indicate employment effects ranging from −6 percent to +1 percent, with midpoint estimates of around −2.5 percent for both female-dominated and other jobs.

In sum it appears that however we group occupations, we find fairly small employment effects of around −3 percent from our predicted comparable worth wage adjustments, although some of the upper-bound estimates are substantial. Of course, employment declines for particular jobs with close substitutes and relatively large comparable worth wage increases could be considerably larger than these estimates indicate.

COMBINED EMPLOYMENT EFFECTS

How much would comparable worth be likely to reduce female employment? We have estimated that the likely increase in women's relative wages within occupations would reduce female employment within such jobs by perhaps 1 percent (right-hand column of Table 6–2) and the likely increase in wages of female-dominated jobs would reduce employment in them around 2.5 percent. Together, this suggests that employment of women in female-dominated jobs might fall by around 3.5 percent. Obviously, this is a very rough estimate, both because the models and data employed to derive it are barely adequate to the task and also because different assumptions about the effect of these wage increases on the total wage bill generate a fairly wide range of estimates.

THE IMPACT OF EMPLOYMENT CHANGES ON WOMEN'S EARNINGS

Although comparable worth might result in measurable declines in women's employment, it seems fairly clear that it would raise their total earnings (number of workers times wages) even after adjusting for employment effects, and it would raise their share of the wage bill.

Table 5–4 presented evidence that comparable worth applied to all jobs would raise women's wages by 13.8 percent and men's by 2.5 percent. Thus, in a "typical" occupation, women would experience a wage increase of nearly 14 percent and an employment decline of about 3.5 percent. As a result, their aggregate earnings would rise by about 10 percent, or roughly three-fourths as much as their wages. In addition, as the figures in Table 6–1 suggest, the elasticity of substitution of female for male workers within an occupation is less than one and probably around .35. If comparable worth were to raise women's *relative* wages by 11.3 percent, an elasticity of substitution of .35 implies that their relative employment will decline by about 4 percent and so their share of that occupation's wage bill will rise.

Similarly, the equations in Part A of Table 6–4 imply that the share of the wage bill going to workers in female-dominated jobs would rise as a result of our estimated comparable worth wage adjustment. Since

$$S_2 = -.221\ln W_1 + .221\ln W_2$$

then

$$\Delta S_2 = -.221(\%\Delta W_1) + .221(\%\Delta W_2)$$
$$= .221(\%\Delta W_2 - \%\Delta W_1)$$

If wages were to rise by 13.6 percent in female-dominated jobs and 3.6 percent in other jobs, as our estimates suggest, the share of female jobs in the wage bill would rise about 2.2 percentage points. In short, while the disemployment effects of comparable worth would surely harm some individuals, they would raise the earnings of women as a group and would raise the share going to female jobs.

CONCLUSION

This chapter has assembled disparate pieces of evidence on the possible employment effects of the comparable worth wage adjustments estimated in the preceding chapter. Though our own estimates are crude and the U.S. minimum wage experience and Australian comparable worth experiment only roughly apply to the case at hand, we can draw some encouragement from the consistency of all these results. Our broad conclusion is that we may expect small but not negligible employment effects from any significant comparable worth wage increase. Thus, our findings corroborate neither the advocate's assertion quoted at the outset of this chapter that "there's no evidence that jobs will be lost" nor the critic's view that there would be "massive dislocations." Moreover, we find that comparable worth would probably raise the total earnings (as well as the hourly wages) of all women and especially those in female jobs. As is usual in economic matters, when partisan claims are put to the test the results are far less dramatic than either camp would have us believe.

NOTES

1. Employers have long used piece rates to motivate worker productivity, and the scientific management movement that began around the turn of the century stressed that a properly implemented system of incentive pay could raise productivity and wages while lowering labor costs (Montgomery 1979). The most famous exponent of the high-wage/low-labor-cost theory of wages was Henry Ford I. Ford preached this doctrine in several books (Ford 1923, 1926), and he put it into practice in 1914 by setting a $5.00 minimum daily wage in his Highland Park factory at the same time he reduced the work day to eight hours. Ford's motives for this move were complex, but they apparently included the hope that it would reduce labor turnover—which had average 370 percent during 1912 and 1913 (Ford 1923, 1926; Nevins 1954; Meyer 1981).
2. The literature on companies' internal efficiency and its determinants is enormous. For assessments and references to the most important findings, see any good industrial organization text such as Scherer (1980: Ch. 17) and Greer (1984: Ch. 19).
3. This section relies heavily on Gregory and Duncan (1981).
4. We note that Gregory and Duncan interpret their own findings quite differently than we have here and that their conclusions have been widely cited as evidence that comparable worth has had no adverse employment effect in Australia.
5. Due to sample size limitations we were forced to combine the clerical and the sales and service categories that were treated separately in Chapter 5. Because our labor categories are so aggregative and because the models estimated below also contain no measure of capital services or any other nonlabor input, the

results of this section must again be taken as very rough estimates of the possible employment effects reported below.

6. This equation appears in Ehrenberg and Smith (1984). It is derived in the following manner. The share of any given occupation in the firm's total employment budget is

$$S_i = W_iE_i/\Sigma_j W_j E_j$$

Taking the natural log of this and differentiating it while holding the employment budget constant yields

$\Delta lnS_i = \Delta lnW_i + \Delta lnE_i$ or roughly

$\Delta S_i/S_i = \%\Delta W_i + \%\Delta E_i$ (1)

From the translog specification we know that

$$S_i = \Sigma_j a_{ij}lnW_j$$

Hence

$\Delta S_i = \Sigma_j a_{ij}\Delta lnW_j$ or

$\Delta S_i = \Sigma_j a_{ij}\%\Delta W_j$ (2)

Substituting (2) into (1) and rearranging the terms results in

$$\%\Delta E_i = [(1/S_i) \Sigma_j a_{ij}\%\Delta W_j] - \%\Delta W_i$$

which is equation (6.8) in the text.

BIBLIOGRAPHY

Allen, R. G. D. 1938. *Mathematical Analysis for Economists*. New York: St. Martin's Press.

Anderson, Mary. 1925. "Should There Be Labor Laws for Women? Yes." *Good Housekeeping* (Sept.):53 +.

Berndt, Ernst R., and David O. Wood. 1975. "Technology, Prices, and the Derived Demand for Energy." *The Review of Economics and Statistics* 57 (August):259–68.

Brown, Charles; C. Gilroy; and A. Kohen. 1982. "The Effect of the Minimum Wage on Employment and Unemployment." *Journal of Economic Literature* 20 (June):487–528.

Cherry, Robert. 1982. "Textbook Treatments of Minimum Wage Legislation." Unpublished.

Dorr, Rheta Childe. 1925. "Should There Be Labor Laws for Women? No." *Good Housekeeping* (Sept.):52 +.

Ehrenberg, Ronald, and Robert Smith. 1984. "Comparable Worth in the Public Sector." *NBER Working Paper* 1471. Cambridge, Mass.

Freeman, Richard, and James Medoff. 1982. "Substitution between Production Labor and Other Inputs in Unionized and Non-Unionized Manufacturing." *Review of Economics and Statistics* 64 (May):220–33.

Ford, Henry. 1923. *My Life and Work*. New York: Doubleday.

―――. 1926. *Today and Tomorrow*. New York: Doubleday.

Greer, Douglas. 1984. *Industrial Organization and Public Policy*. 2d ed. New York: Macmillan.

Gregory, R. G., and R. C. Duncan. 1981. "Segmented Labor Market Theories and the Australian Experience of Equal Pay for Women." *Journal of Post-Keynesian Economics* 3 (Spring):403–28.

Hammermesh, Daniel, and James Grant. 1979. "Econometric Studies of Labor–Labor-Substitution and Their Implications for Policy." *Journal of Human Resources* 14 (Fall):518–42.

Meyer, Stephen. 1981. *The Five Dollar Day*. Albany: State University of New York.

Montgomery, David. 1979. *Worker's Control in America*. New York: Cambridge University Press.

Nevins, Allen. 1954. *Ford: The Times, the Man, the Company*. New York: Charles Scribner's Sons.

Peterson, John M. 1959. "Employment Effects of State Minimum Wages for Women, Three Historical Cases Reexamined." *Industrial and Labor Relations Review* 12 (April):408–22.

Scherer, Fredric M. 1980. *Industrial Market Structure and Economic Performance*. Boston: Houghton Mifflin.

Wall Street Journal. 1982–1985.

CHAPTER 7

Conclusion

[Comparable worth is] pregnant with the possibility of disrupting the entire economic system of the United States/
-JUDGE FRED WINNER in *Lemons v. City and County of Denver* *(New York Times,* Oct. 26, 1979:A20)

The fight against comparable worth must become a top priority for the next Administration.
-THE HERITAGE FOUNDATION, "Mandate for leadership" *(New York Times,* Dec. 3, 1984:A1)

In a market economy, reform movements almost inevitably take the form of restraints on individuals' market activities. In this century the ostensible purpose of most U.S. reform that has impinged on labor markets has been to improve the equity of their operation. But so powerful is the market ethos that reformers almost always claim efficiency benefits for their causes as well. Thus, turn-of-the-century reformers intervened in labor markets to regulate wages, hours, and working conditions for women and children and justified these actions by appeals both to morality and social efficiency. Likewise, contemporary comparable worth advocates who equate "pay equity" with equal returns to skill, effort, and responsibility arrange a convenient marriage of equity and efficiency.

Critics have charged that comparable worth is the modern version of the medieval "just price." But this ignores the central role of job evaluation in comparable worth, and job evaluation is a modern, not a medieval, idea. The roots of comparable worth thus lie less in the middle ages than in the late nineteenth-century social engineering movement. The early social engineers had a vision in which behavioral science would be marshalled in the service of reforms that would enhance both equity and social efficiency. Science provided the evidence that justified the reformer's vision. Since the studies were "scientific," they served to obscure the fact that the reformers' policies would also—by no coincidence—transfer power from groups that had it (such as corporations and political bosses) to those that sought it (the reformers).

Likewise, the technical apparatus of comparable worth—job evaluation and regression analysis—plays an important role in justifying the wage adjustments sought by its advocates. But, as the response of the business community has shown, it has not hidden the power shift that comparable worth would engender. Certainly the technical apparatus of comparable worth cannot be thought revolutionary. Indeed, as we have noted, job evaluation was introduced by employers as a way of securing greater control in the work place. Similarly, regression techniques such as those used above are a widely accepted approach to the analysis of male/female wage differentials. Moreover, application of these commonplace techniques suggests that comparable worth would raise wages in female-dominated jobs by something on the order of 10 to 15 percent, at most.[1] This hardly makes comparable worth seem like a policy conceived in the Politbureau and hardly justifies the dire predictions that the comparable worth movement has evoked from its opponents.

In our view there exists sound evidence that pay discrimination against workers in female-dominated jobs reduces their wages by around 10 to 15 percent. This figure is lower than some comparable worth advocates have claimed because occupational segregation accounts for considerably less of the male/female wage gap than most advocates appear to believe. We conclude, therefore, that a comparable worth wage correction that raises the wages of workers in female-dominated jobs by 10 to 15 percent would in most instances be a blow for pay equity and a move toward efficient, nondiscriminating labor markets. Such a wage increase should be seen as a redress for job segregation rather than as an unwarranted intervention in efficient labor markets.

But to see comparable worth as nothing other than a technique that would simply correct for discrimination is to miss its true significance. The real threat of comparable worth to the business community lies in its challenge to managerial wage-setting prerogatives. Perhaps an analogy with the environmental movement will help. Although the Environmental Protection Agency (EPA) and Occupational Safety and Health Administration (OSHA) have imposed some real costs on the private sector, the hostility they have provoked in the business community cannot be understood in these terms alone. These agencies have also transferred some control over costs and production decisions (the choice of technology and the organization of work) from business managers to federal agencies. Fundamental decisions about what, where, and how a firm produces have become matters for lawyers to determine at administrative hearings, and to an affected business the outcome becomes uncontrolled and unpredictable.

Similarly, comparable worth as a public policy would transfer the power to set wages for individual jobs from business to the regulatory arena. As we have shown, job evaluation as presently practiced is profoundly arbitrary, and econometric studies can also generate a wide range of comparable worth wage adjustments, depending on the model and controls employed. Thus, while we estimate that a comparable worth correction for wage discrimination in female-dominated jobs would raise wages in these jobs by around 10 to 15 percent and while the actual adjustments made by various state and local governments where comparable worth has been implemented have been on this same order of magnitude, there is no guarantee that prescribed wage corrections would be this small in all instances. More importantly, if comparable worth advocates obtained the power to set or otherwise regulate wages, they would presumably use that power to gain the biggest wage increases they could get for their constituency. Ultimately, wages or rules for setting wages are determined by the relative power of employers and employees (constrained, of course, by external labor and product market conditions), and comparable worth threatens to shift power away from employers in this distributional conflict.

This argument suggests that the threat of comparable worth to the business community rises with the level of government that implements it. As a private policy advocated by labor unions and pursued exclusively through collective bargaining, comparable worth amounts to nothing more than a new issue injected into wage negotiations. In this context it does not challenge the *rules* by which wages are set. Ultimately its impact would depend on the relative bargaining power of employers and the unions they are negotiating with and would be constrained by market conditions. This is something with which most employers have learned to live. As a policy required of state and local government employers, comparable worth would still be a relative minor threat, raising market wages somewhat in affected jobs and serving to legitimize the comparable worth demands of private sector employees. State and local governments' ability to impose comparable worth on private employers in their jurisdiction would be severely circumscribed by a firm's ability to escape to jurisdictions with more favorable business climates, however.

But as federal policy, a comparable worth law would face greatly attenuated constraints. Although current bills would apply only to federal agencies and contractors, federal comparable worth legislation is feared by businesses as a stalking horse for future legislation that would apply to private employers as well. It is at this level that the spector of comparable worth haunts the business community, threatening a significant curtailment of employers' wage-setting prerogatives and a highly politicized free-for-all over the distribution of income.

NOTES

1. Recall that this is an upper-bound estimate and that it is based on national, rather than firm, data. In fact, any conceivable U.S. comparable worth law would apply only within firms, and a comparable worth law that applied at the level of the individual firm would not adjust for the interfirm wage differences reflected in our data. We therefore view our 10 to 15 percent estimate of the comparable worth wage increase in women's jobs to be higher than what we would expect to find within a typical establishment.

BIBLIOGRAPHY

New York Times. 1979–1984.

INDEX

Abram, Morris, 46
AFL-CIO, 29, 43
Apples and oranges, 109–110
American Federation of Government
  Employees, 32
American Federation of State, County
  and Municipal Employees (AFSCME),
  41, 43–44, 48
AFSCME v. State of Washington, 48–51
American Federation of Teachers, 32
Anderson, Mary, 158
Australia, comparable worth in, 159–160

Becker, Gary, 79, 85–86
Bennett amendment, 47–48
  Narrowed in *Gunther*, 48
  See also Civil Rights Act of 1964
Bergmann, Barbara, 81
Black Workers
  Impact of comparable worth wage
    adjustment on, 58–60, 133, 143,
    146–149
  Impact of World War I on, 13
Blau, Francine, 130
Blue Collar Jobs
  Impact of comparable worth on wages
    in, 133, 139, 142, 148–149
  Impact of comparable worth on
    employment in, 165
  Percent female in, 134–135
  Wages in, 16, 57, 134–135
Brady Dorothy, 24
Brown, Randall, Marilyn Moon and
  Barbara Zolith, 92
Buchele, Robert, 92

Census Bureau
  Data on wage gap, xix, 27
  Data on women's jobs and wages,
    134–135, 150–152
Chaikin, Sol, 43
Civil Rights Act of 1964, xix, 47–50
  Impact on women's jobs and wages, 30
  Relation to Equal Pay Act, 47–48
Clerical jobs. *See* White collar jobs
Commission on Civil Rights, role in
  comparable worth cases, 46, 50

Communications Workers of America, 43
Comparable worth
  Advocate's Model, 113–119
  Affinity for public sector, 41
  Australian experience with, 159–160
  Benefits to middle class, 133, 149
  Black workers and, 143, 146–149
  Blue collar workers and, 139, 142,
    148–149
  Correction for discrimination, 60–62,
    100, 117
  Criticisms of, 60–63, 70–71, 95, 109–112,
    130 n.7
  Definitions of, 62, 72, n.4, 108–111, 116,
    119, 136;
  Economist's Model, 119–124; wage
    adjustments in, 120–124, 127–128,
    136–143, 152 n.3 and n.4;
  Employer hostility, 41–42, 45, 174–176
  Employment effects of: in Australia
    159–160; within jobs, 160–162;
    between jobs, 162–167; in
    female-dominated jobs, 168; in total,
    168
  Federal, state and local initiatives, 41,
    43–45, 64–69
  Historical origins, xx, 29–33
  Impact on Individuals' earnings,
    143–146
  Impact on wage gap, 143
  Job choice, effect on comparable worth
    wage adjustment, 124–127
  Legal status of, 45–51; requirement of
    equal jobs, 47
  Occupational earnings, impact on:
    136–143; in female-dominated jobs,
    137–142; in public sector jobs,
    137–139; effect on men's earnings,
    139–142
  Politics of, 40–51, 63
  Theory of, 105–109
  Unions and, 31–33, 41–45; in collective
    bargaining, 43–45
  White collar workers and, 135, 139, 142,
    148–149
Compensating wage differential, 57–58,
  106–107, 114–115, 119, 130 n.10, 131 n.12

Constant elasticity of substitution
production function, 160–162
Crowding, 82, 84
Impact on compensating wage
differential, 106
Cowley, Geoffrey, 46

Denver Nurses. *See Lemons v. City and
County of Denver*
Dictionary of Occupational Titles, 59,
70–71, 90, 94–95
Factor analysis of variables in, 125–126
Discrimination in Labor Markets, 48,
76–84
Theories of, 79–84
Comparable worth as correction for,
117
Disparate impact, 49, 72 n.1
Dorr, Rhetta Childe, 157–158
Douglas, Hellen Gahagen, 25
Duncan Index, 2–3
D-value, 79–81, 85–86

Earnings gap. *See* Wage gap
Ehrenberg, Ronald and Robert Smith,
162, 171 n.6
Elasticity of Demand for Labor
Constant output, 161, 165
Constant wage bill, 165, 168, 171 n.6
Elasticity of Substitution
And the impact of comparable worth
on women's share of the wage bill,
169
Of male for female workers in
Australia, 159
Of male for female workers within jobs
in United States, 160–162
Relationship to elasticity of demand for
labor and employment, 161, 165, 171
n.6
Employment effects of comparable worth
Between jobs, 162–167
On female-dominated jobs, 168
On women's earnings, 169
Within jobs, 160–162
England, Paula, 84–85; and Marilyn
Chassie and Linda McCormack, 94
Equal Employment Opportunity
Commission
AFSCME files charges with, 44
Comparable worth ruling, 46, 50
Equal opportunity, Progressives
uninterested in, 7
Equal Pay
Acts of 1946–1948, 24–26
Act of 1963, xix, 29–30, 46–48; relation
to Civil Rights Act, 47–48

During wartime, 14, 22–23
State Laws on, 24, 29, 64–69

Factor scores, as measures of job
requirements, 95
Female-dominated jobs
Evidence on, 134–135, 150–152
Impact of comparable worth adjustment
on employment in, 168–169
Impact of comparable worth adjustment
on wages in, 137–142, 146
See also Percent female
Ferraro, Mike, 44
Filer, Randall, 124
Fortune magazine, 21
Freeman, Richard, and Jonathan Leonard,
32

General educational development, as job
requirement, 95
General Order 16. *See* War Labor Board
Gini coefficient, impact of comparable
worth on, 144–146, 149
See also Comparable worth: Impact on
individuals' earnings; Wage gap
Glass industry, wage gap in during
Progressive era, 8–11
Goodell, Charles, 29–30
Gregory, R. C. and R. G. Duncan,
159–160, 170 n.4
Griggs v. Duke Power, 72 n.1

Hay Associates, 44, 54–63, 70–71, 72 n.2
Hildebrand, George, 46
Horowitz, Michael, 133
Human capital
As explanation for male-female wage
gap, xx, 8–9, 18, 23, 39–31
Interaction with percent female in
occupations, 98
Men's and women's levels of, xx, 18,
29–30, 80, 91
Returns to, 18, 22–24, 29, 31, 77–79, 81,
83, 94, 101 n.1, 111, 129

Indifference curves, 77, 106
Industrial segregation, 5
Lack of connection to wage gap, 16–17
Impact of World War II on, 21–24
International Ladies Garment Workers, 43
International Union of Electrical Workers,
25, 43
Iso-profit curves, 77, 106
Job Evaluation
Critiques of, 54–60, 112
Point factor method, 51–56; weighting
of factors, 52, 57–60; linking pay to
factor points, 53–54

Race bias, 58–60
Role in comparable worth studies,
49–54
Sex bias, 52–54, 56–57
Scientific management and, 26, 173–174
White collar bias, 52–53, 57–60

Job Traits, returns to, 60–62, 70–71, 72
n.3, 101 n.1, 106–108, 111–112, 114–116,
120
Johnson, George and Gary Solon, 119
Jones, F. L., 70
Jusenius, Carol, 88

Killingsworth, Mark, 112
Krauthammer, Charles, 54–55

Labor unions
Female membership, 32–33, 42–45
Legal access to company race and sex
data, 43
Support for comparable worth, 25, 29,
31–33, 41–45
Support for early protective legislation,
8
Laissez faire, reformers rejection of, 7, 12,
31
Lemons v. City and County of Denver, 47
Levin, Michael, 46

Madden, Janice, 82
Men's wages, impact of comparable
worth on, 139–142, 148
Men's and women's jobs
Defined, 113, 130 n.3; arbitrariness of,
118–119
Job requirements as cause of wage
differences, 70–71, 124, 127
Middle class, 12
Benefits from comparable worth, 133,
149
Minimum wage
Employment effects in theory, 155–157;
evidence of, 12, 158–159
Reformers' views on, 20, 157–158
Monopoly in labor markets, 82
Monopsony in labor markets, 11, 82–83,
156
Mueller v. Oregon, 12

National Academy of Science
Review of job evaluation. See Treiman,
Donald
Study of Comparable Worth. See
Treiman, Donald, and Heidi
Hartmann
National Labor Relations Board v.
Westinghouse Electric Corp, 43

National Longitudenal Surveys, 95
Representativeness of data, 98, 152
n.1
National Recovery Act, 20
Newmann, Winn, 57
Significance of AFSCME v. State of
Washington, 49
Niemi, Albert, 18
Ninth Circuit Court of Appeals, 50
Niskanen, William, 54, 57

Occupational distribution
Cause of wage gap. See Occupational
segregation.
Job choice as a determinant of, 9, 84,
124–127
Models of, 92
Occupational segregation
Cause of wage gap, 16–17, 27–28,
84–99; comparable worth advocates'
views, 85–87; critique of evidence,
87–94; interfirm differences, 130
n.6
Measurement of, 2–3
Theory of discrimination as cause of,
79–84
Trends in: to World War I, 3–6; World
War I to 1929, 13–18; 1930–1945,
18–24; 1945 on, 27–29
Occupational skill requirements, 77
Occupation wage equations
Heteroscedasticity, 102
In advocates model of comparable
worth, 114–116
In economist's model of comparable
worth, 119–120
Returns to job traits, 76–79, 98, 101 n.1,
106, 111–112; in comparable worth
correction, 108, 116, 120
To estimate effect of occupational
segregation, 95–99

Pay equity. See Comparable worth
Pendleton, Clarence, 54, 133
Percent female in occupation
As compensible job trait, 107
As proxy for working conditions, 126
Impact on occupational wages, 93–94,
97–99
In Census occupations, 134–135,
150–152
In economist's model, 119
See also Female-dominated jobs; Men's
and women's jobs
Point factor method. See Job evaluation
Polachek, Soloman, 84
Professional and technical jobs. See White
collar jobs

Progressivism
Concern with women workers, 1, 6–8, 12–13, 20, 26, 31, 34
Parallels with comparable worth movement, 1, 12–13, 173–174
Protective legislation, 7–8, 12–13
Public sector jobs, impact of comparable worth on, 137–139

Remick, Helen, 54, 56, 86, 111
Reskin, Barbara, 86
Roemer, Ruth, 25
Roos, Paula, 92–93

Sales and service workers. *See* White collar jobs
Service Employees International Union, 32
Silk industry, wage gap during progressive era, 8–11
Specific vocational preparation, as job requirement, 95
Steinberg, Ronnie, 45; and Lois Haignere, 56
Stevenson, Mary, 90–91
Supply and demand, 62–63, 110–112

Tanner, Jack. *See AFSCME v. State of Washington*
Title VII. *See* Civil Rights Act of 1964; Bennett amendment
Translog cost function
Estimation of, 164–165
Used to predict employment change for occupations, 165–168, 171 n.6
Treiman, Donald, 56
Treiman, Donald and Heidi Hartmann, 88–90, 93
Treiman, Donald, Heidi Hartmann and Paula Roos, 73 n.3, 93–94

Wage Gap between men and women
Effect of percent female in occupation on, 98–99

Explanations for, xx, 8–9, 31
Comparable worth, impact on, 143, 146, 149, 169, 174
Impact of working conditions and job choice on, 124–127
Occupational segregation as a cause of, 2–4, 9–11, 16–18, 23–24, 27–28; evidence and criticism, 84–99; comparable worth advocates' views, 85–87; within firms, 130 n.7
Partitioning, 60–62, 70–71
Theories of discrimination as cause, 80–81
Trends in: to World War I, 3–5; World War I to 1929, 13–18; 1930 to 1945, 18–24; 1945 on, xix–xxi, 27–29
War Labor Board, 22
Washington County, Oregon v. Gunther, 42–49
Intentional sex discrimination in, 48
Weidenbaum, Murray, 45
White collar jobs, xix, 5–6, 11–12, 16, 18, 31
Employment impact of comparable worth on, 165
Motivation for comparable worth in, xix, 31, 57–58
Percent female in, 134–135
Wage impact of comparable worth on, 139, 142, 148–149
Wages in, 134–135
Williamson, Jeffery and Peter Lindert, 23, 29
Willis, Normal B. and Associates, 54–63
Women's Bureau, 20, 25, 158
Women's Jobs and wages, Census data on, 134–135, 150–152
See also Men's and women's jobs; Female-dominated jobs; Wage gap
World War I, 13–14
World War II, 21–23
Works Progress Administration, 20–21

ABOUT THE AUTHORS

Mark Aldrich was born in Northampton, Massachusetts, in 1941. He attended Middlebury College, receiving a bachelor's degree in history. He earned a master's degree in economics from the University of California at Berkeley and a Ph.D. in economics from the University of Texas at Austin. Dr. Aldrich has taught economics at Smith College since 1968. During 1979–80 and 1982–83, he worked as a senior economist in the Office of Regulatory Analysis at the Occupational Safety and Health Administration in Washington, D.C., and has consulted for that agency and for the Economic Development Administration. His previous books include an economic analysis of technical education in pre–Civil War America and a history of public works in the United States. He has written articles on regulation and economic history most recently on the role of women in the U.S. work force.

Robert Buchele has taught economics at Smith College since 1977. His fields are labor economics, income distribution, and econometrics. He is also director of the Jahnige Social Science Research Center at Smith. He was raised in Los Angeles and studied engineering at UCLA. Dr. Buchele holds a master's degree in management from MIT and a Ph.D. in economics from Harvard University. He has taught at the University of Massachusetts in Amherst and Boston and worked as a CETA consultant evaluating job training and public service employment programs in western Massachusetts. Dr. Buchele's previous publications include articles on comparable worth, race and sex discrimination, and labor market segmentation.